Chewing the Page

The Mourning Goats Interviews

Chewing the Page

The Mourning Goats Interviews

Phil Jourdan

(editor) and The Goat

(editor/interviewer)

PERFECT
EDGE
BOOKS

Winchester, UK
Washington, USA

First published by Perfect Edge Books, 2013
Perfect Edge Books is an imprint of John Hunt Publishing Ltd., Laurel House, Station Approach,
Alresford, Hants, SO24 9JH, UK
office1@jhpbooks.net
www.johnhuntpublishing.com
www.perfectedgebooks.com

For distributor details and how to order please visit the 'Ordering' section on our website.

ISBN: 978 1 78099 589 2

Design: Stuart Davies

Printed in the USA by Edwards Brothers Malloy

We operate a distinctive and ethical publishing philosophy in all
areas of our business, from our global network of authors to
production and worldwide distribution.

CONTENTS

Editor's Introduction

The Goat — that is his name — started a website to post some interviews with authors. They were good interviews. Each author had to answer twenty questions, and then the interview went up. After a year of this, the Goat had accumulated enough material for a collection in print, and we decided to go for it.

I had been one of his interviewees, and I liked his style. He asks simple questions. The Goat is not a pretentious interviewer, and if these interviews are a great read, it's because he doesn't get invasive or try to be too clever. Just twenty questions about how his favorite authors work their magic. Twenty questions isn't a huge number, but it's enough for you to get to know how these different artists work.

For this print edition we've expanded many of the interviews. Most participants were happy to elaborate on their answers. We've also included a brand new five-question interview.

The point of this collection is to help writers discover how authors like Stephen Graham Jones, Craig Clevenger, Lidia Yuknavitch, Nick Hornby, and many, many others do their job.

I hope you enjoy the Goat's company.

— Phil Jourdan

Introduction: Confessions of The Goat

On www.mourninggoats.com you'll find the nice and simple reasons why I started the Mourning Goats interviews, but for the book, I want to come clean on the more sinister origins of all of this. You're probably now thinking, Goat, it's a blog on which you ask authors twenty questions, how sinister can it be? And, for the most part, I agree, but there are levels of deceit, right?

First sinister confession! I am not a goat. I know. A lot of you are picturing a majestic, cloven-hoofed animal, teetering on the edge of a mountain to access the Internet on a shoddy Macintosh computer with a satellite modem. The computer you see was passed down from a time when color computer screens and 1+ gig video cards were thought of by only the most tech-savvy hopefuls. But alas, I do not live near the mountains or type the questions with hooves. I'm just a guy who enjoys reading good fiction and tries his damnedest to write his own.

Second sinister confession! I have two reasons for always asking the same first question: What comes to mind when you hear Mourning Goats? When I was writing the very first interview with Stephen Elliott, I thought to myself, what are all of these authors going to think of such a silly name for an author interview site? I mean, it's not Writer's Digest, The Bookslut, Goodreads, LitReactor, or Booked and the name doesn't have anything to do with literature. How are these people going to respond to questions from a weirdo with a goat fetish? (So far, quite well.) The second reason, and I believe the more important, was because I wanted new fiction from my favorite authors. Its just that simple. Go read Michael Kun's answer to understand what I mean.

Third and final sinister confession! At the heart of the site, the most heinous reason I started it, was to steal the tricks of all of my favorite authors. I've been writing for years without much success, and I kept asking myself why. What do these seemingly normal people have that I don't? Is it where they grew up? Is it their education? Maybe it's what they write on. Maybe it's because they outline their work. Maybe it's because they don't. I kept asking questions and started to realize what all these authors had in common. They all went for it. Yes, they had talent, but they didn't wait for inspiration to hit. They didn't wait for someone to come to them and say, here's your book deal! Congratulations! They wrote, sometimes a ridiculous amount, and sent it out. If the stories were rejected, they wore their rejections on their chest like medals. The whole time, their trick was just hard work.

Writing twenty questions about someone you know is hard, writing twenty questions about someone you've never met but who's told you a story is even harder. I could easily reveal my name here and on the front of the book, but instead, I want you to focus on what's inside. It's the authors that I want you to see, not the interviewer. All fiction is a bunch of lies trying to prove themselves, and I'm just a goat trying to show off some of my favorite liars.

Thank you,

Goat

Stephen Graham Jones

What comes to mind when you hear "Mourning Goats?"

Mourning Doves, the 'goats of morning,' which is, I don't know — regret? Morning Glories too, a plant that's always confused me. Or, in this novel I just wrote, The Gospel of Z, there's these goats in it, which could definitely be said to be mourning. Saddest goats ever. Don't even want to be thinking about them. Except I love them, also. And then I guess I somehow spider over to that old strange short film, "Adonis XIV," maybe it was called? Exterminating Angel kind of stuff. With this ram. Probably one of the more influential things I've seen, now that I actually think about it. Have never shaken that movie off. Not sure I want to.

It Came from Del Rio came out on the 23rd of October and The Ones That Got Away came out the 16th of November, the same year. While teaching full-time, how do you find the time to write?

Man, for me it's more like, how do I find the time to stay sane. Which is to say that writing, for me, it's just trying to make the world make sense. Be that with bunny-headed zombies or insurance office politics or whatever. Writing for me's making this plastic world up, thinking I can play in it, do whatever I want, have some fun maybe, except then, before I can help it, there's all this real stuff happening, I'm stuck back in a corner, and all I have to get out of this place anymore's a pen. I keep thinking I'm going to 'graduate' as a novelist someday, and have this arm-length distance between me and the stuff on the page, where I can just move it around like chess pieces, analyze this event, that angle, be all objective and longseeing. Have a monocle and cane too, while I'm at it, yeah. But no, no such luck on that kind of distance so far. It's why I write fast, really, because these stories, they always get that bad kind of real to me, where I'm dreaming them, where I'm losing the lines between them and not-them, and so I type faster and faster, trying every door. And then, when I finally get out, I feel great for a week, maybe even two weeks, I'm happy, the world's divided up as it should be between things that happen and things that I know can't be happening, but then, yeah, then I'm sitting on some bad-idea bench in a worse place I only meant to walk through, and I'm writing down . . . not a premise for a story, those are easy, but a voice that wants to tell a story. If I listen to it too long, too, then I'm back inside another book, going as fast as I can. Wash rinse repeat.

However, I don't mean to be all romantic about writing either, don't want to set it up as 'the lonely, tortured novelist battles x amount of demons, reaches into the fire to pull this story out,' any of that. I mean, I see people everyday doing real work. It makes me completely aware that writing, it's hardly real work. It's fun work, I just always fall too deep into it. Or jump, yeah. With never any idea how deep this is going to get this time.

I loved your short story book, Bleed into Me, so I'm really looking forward to The Ones That Got Away, also, the description of It Came From Del Rio sounds amazing, what can you tell us about the two?

In that order, The Ones That Got Away, it's all horror stories. Stuff that really and truly scares me. I'm always telling my students that you can render no emotional landscape you haven't, to some degree at least, experienced. It's how you know those contours, the slope and sway of the land, can make it real for your reader. But that's not to say that you've got to go on some murder spree in order to write like Chelsea Cain, either. However, we have all — 'to some degree' — destroyed another person, yes? Effectively, figuratively at least, 'killed' them. Be it your mom, disappointed you stole the earrings her first, real husband gave her (and her never outing you), or a dog you accidentally caught with your bumper, whose five-year-old owner you could see standing in their lawn in your rear view mirror. I mean, that, that's horror to me, and I guess that's the vein I was tapping in The Ones That Got Away. The scary things, finally, they're not the slobbering toothed beasties in the shadows, they're the decisions we make, and then have to live with. Or try to live with. But this isn't at all to say that there aren't Old West zombies and Near Dark vampires and ghosts and worse in Ones. There are, and more. But there's also rabbits and gas pumps and high schools. There's our world, this world, the place we live, wrapped around this terrible, terrible stuff. And people trying to make it through to the other side. And, if I had to cite any influences for this collection, it'd have to be a combo of King and Ketchum, maybe. Or, when I think horror, the stuff that's formative for me, that I'm trying to do each time I have a blank page before me, I'm back in The Girl Next Door, as much as I'd never want to be. I'm back in "The Jaunt," my hair turning white in the space of that crossing.

For It Came From Del Rio, though, man, I think I'd just found Joe R. Lansdale when I wrote that. Mike Shea at Texas Monthly had told me I should really look some of his stuff up. So thankful for that rec. Lansdale's stuff, the confidence and ease with which he tells his stories, it's — I wanted to say infectious, but, really, like with Vonnegut, it's intimidating. But if you can get over that, you can maybe write a novel set down on the Texas border, with a dad come back from the dead, a dad whose own head kind of wears out, so he has to do what people on the border do: improvise. Find a giant bunny, take its head. The obvious solution, really. And, yeah, I mean, there's meteor radiation, there's chupacabras — I'm so fascinated by those dog-things that were showing up back then — there's revenge and reconciliation, and, because I'd just been reading Dracula and Frankenstein, it's epistolary too. And I guess probably nostalgic as well, as I used to live down around Austin, a little place called Wimberley, and for a lot of years in a row I was always hitting the Texas Book

Festival, but somehow, probably because I usually flew in, I never made it back out there. When I'd been there it had been eighth grade for me, I mean, so, my memory of it's eighth-grade, and all the eighth-grade magical stuff that's going on, that you don't want to mess up by seeing from an adult angle. Maybe I was afraid to go back there, could only go back as a bunny-headed zombie. Sounds ridiculous, but that may actually be it. Well, that and my wife at the time was telling me that I never wrote any love stories. So, with Del Rio, I kind of tried, and kind of failed. A book or two later, though — Flushboy and Not for Nothing (Dzanc, 2013, 2014) both — I think I got it closer to right. But, too, ask me and I'll say all my stories are love stories. I'm a complete sap, wholly sentimental. Just, sometimes the love affair's with a truck, or a knife, or a song, or a place. In It Came From Del Rio, that place is South Texas. A big piece of me's always going to be there.

I noticed that the only book you have out on Kindle is Demon Theory, is this a choice or are the others coming? What are your thoughts on e-readers?

Yeah, I hear with Demon Theory the notes are even kind of linked, yeah? That's cool. All for it. I mean, I've got it on my Kindle (felt so loserly, buying my own book, yes), but seem to be very poor at actually paging through it. Same with the audio version: can't really listen. It's too strange. But, no, it's not been a choice for me either way. With Demon Theory, I was surprised when it showed up e-, and audio. And, It Came From Del Rio, Trapdoor's definitely going e- with it — they may just win any e-book wars that happen to happen. Very slick model, they've got. And Kindle (Kindle 2), or its app on my phone, it's by far my preferred way to read. I mean, I'm reading Handling the Undead now, forever after everybody else, solely because it wouldn't be available in digital version. It's why I've yet to read Bolano, too. Paper books to me, they're wonderful treasures, great artifacts, and I like that I can get them wet and use them for stairsteps and doorstops and flykillers, forget them on airplanes, all that, but, when I want to ingest a text, lose myself in the words, then digital's the quickest way to complete immersion. I can go so much faster that way, fast enough, I suspect, that my critical faculties break down the slightest bit, and I'm reading the text at the speed necessary to record it in my head more as an experience. Reading on my Kindle feels so much more vital, anyway. But, no, I can't mark up the text like I'd like, I can't draw unicorns in the margins, I can't read comics, can't hit Wired, any of that coolness. But the tech's making all the necessary strides, I'm sure. And I can draw unicorns in lots of other places for the time being.

It sounds like you're teaching some pretty interesting classes at the University of Colorado, Boulder, what are some of your favorite?

Ridiculous as it sounds, I'm still completely in love with teaching fiction writing. Each and every time, I learn something, the students teach me something. I don't mean each semester, either. More like each class meeting. A complete rush, and wholly a scam that I get paid for it. But shhh. To say it cleaner, I guess, articulating stuff about stories to the students, making it digestible, learnable, it improves my own fiction. And they're not just teaching me what not to do either, of course. A lot of the time they're doing stuff I hadn't even considered.

But, I also teach some lit, and that's a complete blast. I've done the Haunted House — the genre's so elegant — the Slasher, which I needed about fourteen more years in that semester to say everything I wanted to say, and, now, The Zombie. Which, even when I wrote Del Rio, I seriously knew very little about zombies. They liked brains, used to be dead? Okay, check, check. But now, studying all the different flavors of zombie kind, well, first, it's so helpful when talking Del Rio, because now I can see what I was doing, but, second, it's turning out that the zombie genre's just as elegant as the Haunted House, as the Slasher. There's taxonomies

8

and tropes and archetypes and it all matters, is all part of the dynamo that drives the story. Loving it. Hope soon to teach werewolves and vampires. Need to be figuring them out as well. Which — all my lit classes, they're never me walking into the room, having a clutch of answers and some pedagogical vehicle with which to deliver those answers. No, I come in with questions, with "how does this work?," with "why this, not that?," and over the course of the semester we try to tease apart a set of answers. Or, we get our hands bloody, and try to pull something recognizable up from the operating table.

You received your Ph.D. in Creative Writing at Florida State University, in two years; can you explain how you did it so fast, and what your thoughts are on the teaching of creative writing?

Only reason I did my Ph.D that fast was — well, first, it was that I was on University Fellowship, so didn't have to teach, could overload on hours, but, more than that, it was that Florida made me very, very nervous. Let me add another 'very' there. We had a dog back then that needed walking a lot, and so I'd take her on these rambling journeys, me reading the whole time, or, at first, trying to read anyway. But, there were all these freaktacular bugs everywhere, each of which I thought was definitely going to jump on my face, suck my eyeball juice out. And spiders, man, there were webs taller than I was. And, and sometimes I'd stall out at fences, look down these grassy slopes to real true live alligators, little ones just chasing frogs, but watching me as well, telling me 'later, bub. You'. I've never been so terrified. Which — where I hunt, there's grizzly sign everywhere, they're going to sleep later and later these last few years, their tracks on my tracks, blood on their tracks sometimes, me often carrying something dead around, and, yeah, that definitely doesn't not suck, and there's wolves all over too, and just endless trees to freeze to death in, and series of guns in my hand that I don't remotely trust not to shoot me, but, still: it's not Florida. So, I say it was the bugs and the gators and the spiders, and it was, that was what pushed me through FSU so fast, but it was also that Florida was very squishy, very green. And, I was raised in West Texas, didn't even know how to swim until forever. It was like Dune planet, pretty much. Of course I'm fundamentally terrified of water. Too, though, my biggest dream — okay, aside from space travel with kind of nice aliens — it's to see a real whale. Just surfacing, breathing, rolling back under. Would be completely and absolutely magic. However, closest I've been to being on a real boat's the ferry by the Golden Gate Bridge. Which I rode just to ride, same as I rode the streetcar earlier that day. I didn't see any whales. Was the only one of the whole ferry, I think.

November 1st, is the first day of NANOWRIMO, do you have plans for this year? What's come from these in the past?

I've never NANOWRIMO'd, but I always try to get my students to. I did finish Demon Theory over Thanksgiving in 1999 though, if that can count. But, no, I don't do it. I have done the three-day novel contest a couple of times, though. That's more my speed. First time out I jammed down a hundred and fifty-two pages, I think, but didn't win. Second time, I wrote The Long Trial of Nolan Dugatti, then withdrew it from consideration so Chiasmus could publish it. I'd guess I wrote Del Rio in four or six weeks, too — almost a month? — but Ones, no, that wasn't all at once, was piecemeal, across about five years. I don't see how you can do a collection any other way. You've got to have a lot of misfires, I mean, a lot of tangents so you can figure out what you're maybe really trying to say here.

Social media is everywhere these days, and you have a huge presence on it, how do you think social media is changing the way we communicate, especially the way authors are currently using it?

I think it's allowing us to collapse that distance between author and reader. I get hit up all the time on Facebook, I mean, people telling me their cool stories about finding one of my books, meeting a girl or guy because of it, and, that's what it's about, for me. Sure, cashing a check is nice, but connecting with people — isn't that why we write in the first place? Why I do anyway. I mean, because I rarely can in the meat world. Stick me at a party or a dinner and I won't know what to say, or how to say it, or when to say it, and usually just end up in some story space in the corner, running through junk in my head, trying to crib it down on napkins for later, because I'm going to show all of them.

What are the top five most influential books to your career?

King's It, definitely. Every time I sit down, it's to write that book. And every time, I fail. Erdrich's Love Medicine, too. Have never read a book so true, I don't think. Martel's The Life of Pi, not because it's brilliant, which it is, but because it's got heart. So many books are . . . not afraid to try to connect, to reach out, but afraid to try, have it not work out. Like not telling a joke because you think it might not be funny, yeah? Ketchum's The Girl Next Door, because it's completely unafraid, never looks away, yet also never panders, and has just as much heart as Pi. Maybe more. Love that book. And, a fifth, um, um, okay,The Things They Carried. Probably generic or typical of me to pick that one, but, just because everybody else likes it, does that mean I'm supposed to be cool and say I'm past that? Nope. That book still destroys me, in the way that only fiction can: to build me back up better. And, sixth, since you asked, Vizenor's Bearheart. You know how David Foster Wallace says Blue Velvet was his — his Blue Velvet? In Philip K. Dick terms, his disinhibiting symbol, I guess you could call it, or, talking texts, 'disinhibiting narrative.' Except for DFW it wasn't the actual story, I don't think, it was the singleness of vision, the fidelity to an ethos, something like that. This is what I get from Bearheart: something that's so completely its own thing that it has just a touch more reality than everything else on the shelves.

One of my favorite quotes of yours is, "write yourself into a corner, and give it all away with each line," would you mind

going into more detail, or giving an example in your own writing?

Was just listening to the Farrelly Brothers installment of that screenwriter interview series The Dialogue, with Mike DeLuca — know it? Anyway, they say that too, or one of them does. Was so happy to hear somebody besides me preaching it. But, yeah, if you only write into places you know how to get out of, then you're never going to have to push yourself. Example: Maugham's The Razor's Edge, a kind of oddly compelling book. There's this line about halfway through, something that ends a chapter like "And then the most surprising thing happened." Or "unexpected," something like that. Anyway, man, always do that to yourself, always kill the character you're most attached to, always, if you're Card, burn the Mother Tree, make us think the story's over, that it can't possibly go even one step farther. And then take it all the way around the town. What you're doing is leading your reader into a truly imaginative space, one being created, guessed at, on the fly, one you discover together. It's what real storytelling can be, when it's honest, when it's sincere.

When you write, do you have a daily word count, or page count, or do you just let it flow?

Yeah, I just run as fast as I can, stop only when I have to. I've done forty and more pages a day and I've spent all day on a single paragraph. Never can tell. Maybe someday I'll do the schedule and quota thing, be all grown up like that. Not today, though. Or tomorrow.

Writing is a solitary pastime. Are you a part of any writing groups? Do you have any lucky early readers out there?

I hit up different people I know, yeah, just because the stuff I write, it's not all tailored for a single reader. Well, that's half a lie. She doesn't like it all, or have a taste for it all, but the first and always reader of my stuff's my editor at FC2, Brenda Mills. Every story, every novel, every screenplay, she hits it first. I completely trust what she has to say, not just because she knows her stuff, but because she knows me, knows the stupid stuff I'm always trying to get away with, and calls me on it, and shows me these new and stupider ways I've apparently taken a liking to, and asks if I'm trying to be stupid or does it just come naturally. That kind of stuff. But I can't rely only on her, of course. Just different friends, a lot of them people I've met on-line, even. Smart people. Different people from welcometothevelvet.com, sometimes, or who've hit me up about one thing or another. Christopher O'Riley, a really smart reader, and brilliant musician. My agent, Kate Garric. Nobody from my graduate or undergrad days, though, I guess. Not sure why that is. Maybe my writing's gone a different way from all of them? Not really. I don't know. Never thought about it until now, I don't guess. Three of my brothers, too, they're always good for an early read, will tell me what's what, what's not.

In one interview, I read that you burn a CD and listen to it and only it. While writing each novel, do you still do this? Do you have any other techniques you use in your writing?

Well, I used to do that, yeah. Started with The Fast Red Road, where I had a Marty Robbin's cassette in the player by my computer, would just flip that tape all day, and into the night. But then I figured out CDs somewhat, started doing it like that. Now it's playlists, though, which is completely dangerous, just because there's no 780MB or whatever cap. So the playlist can go on and on, wonderful song after wonderful song, and in just the right order, but it'll take two-plus hours to get through that, too. Which is a long session, at least when you're stealing time from Jim Rockford like I always am. But of course stolen time's the most valuable time, too. The time you can do the most within. Anyway, this most recent playlist, for The Gospel of Z, it's two and half hours.

Once I make it, I never allow myself to take anything out or put anything in. It's done and shut, no do-overs, no exceptions. That is the soundtrack for the novel, whether I regret it or not.

You're very open about your love of horror. What are some of your favorite horror books/movies?

Man, I've hit King and Ketchum above already. I'd add Straub; his Ghost Story and Shadowland are brilliant, plain and simple. And Barker's Damnation Game, say. And I'm just a Barker fanboy, too. Even dug Coldheart Canyon, which I think everybody else hated. And — you read Laird Barron? The precision he jacks his language up to, man. Scary good. And Joe Hill's collection, it was just the medicine horror was needing. I dig bizarro too, but not so much splatterpunk, though Edward Lee, man, he's got it. Is he splatterpunk, though? Not sure. Or, to say all this better: I wish every horror novel could be Robert Marasco's Burnt Offerings. That novel took things up to a height nothing much has hit since, one of those rare instances of story and prose getting into this kind of syncopation that magnified each into so much more.

And, movies, man. Definitely. Scream and Feast are my all-time favorites, of course. And, in spite of how Max Brooks says — correctly, I think — that Return of the Living Dead killed the zombie for twenty years, still, that's so tightly written. How not to love it? And, man, don't get me listing. Dead Snow, Idle Hands, Dead & Breakfast. John Carpenter's The Thing, Nightmare on Elm Street (either, though I guess the first's got a special heart-place). Final Destination 3, The Murder Party, Pontypool, [Rec] (Quarantine too), Boy Eats Girl, Leslie Vernon. Near Dark, always Near Dark. And Terminator, forever, times two. And the fourth Jason. Urban Legend, Identity, House of the Devil, the Orphanage. April Fools Day, Happy Birthday to Me. Harpoon, man, that was a blast and a half. And Halloween, that should be way up front. Anyway, to stop all that: I tend to go for bloody stuff that's got comedy in it. Like Severance. Or the My Bloody Valentine remake. Black Sheep. Shaun of the Dead, yeah. And Trick 'r Treat. Beautiful movie, Trick 'r Treat. And, can Ravenous count as horror? Then Ravenous.

And, talking Ravenous: until I watched the deleted scenes of that movie, I don't think I'd ever trusted an editor, even a little. Always figured they were trying to make me into a hand puppet. But the producers' cuts on Ravenous, and the director's explanations of those cuts, they completely reformed my world. Only other time that's happened, talking fiction at least, is listening to an Art Spiegelman presentation, where all he did was show some long-ago panel cartoonist's rendering of a can of spilled paint. But, right beside it, was an upright can of paint. What Spiegelman said was happening here was that the artist was training us to get the joke, that this was a closed system, one where we understood how a can of paint should be, and how it now was. Such an obvious thing, but one I'd never even had a glimmer of. It completely changed the way I go at writing.

You have a video blog type thing on YouTube, posted by user engldept, do you plan on having more of these?

Yeah, I remember that, I think. I'm wearing a tan jacket, maybe? That jacket was brand new then, years ago. Think I've worn it maybe twice since then. Lately I get all my jackets from Goodwill, and then just never wear those. Much cheaper. Don't think I've watched that clip or interview or video blog, though. Too strange, doing that. But, yeah, I'd guess more stuff'll show up. Probably not recorded by me, as that'd be a crazy trick to pull off, but who knows. Crazy tricks are fun.

On this same video blog, you mention working on a young adult novel with another author. What can you tell us about this? I wouldn't think this would be an area you would be writing in.

Oh, man, I love young adult, just taught a class in it. I read all of it I can. In a lot of ways it's one of the more honest genres, I think. It has something to with how the genre's defined, I think. I mean, romance, western, fantasy, those all have these strict sets of conventions. Not so, YA. YA's more defined by target audience. And, worse, and better, by a target audience that's so much more sophisticated than people, for some reason, assume. So we're getting brilliant stuff like King Dork, say. Or Spanking Shakespeare. Going Bovine, and on and on, I love it all, would so like to be a part of that field. It would be a complete honor. But, I wouldn't even be having that longshot of a chance at that now if Paul Tremblay hadn't called me up a while back, said, hey, what about him and me collaborating on something? I immediately said yes, based solely on having read Paul's stuff. He's a very strong writer, is all the way in control of what he's doing. Wait, not 'solely' — also I know Paul, had hung out with him some, he'd pulled me into an anthology, I think, I blurbed one of his books back before we really knew each other. Anyway, it's completely cool, writing with him. Maybe we'll be like Gaiman and Pratchett, hitting one ball all the way home (or, is that wrong? 'Out of the field?' I know so little about baseball, shouldn't even get to use sports metaphors, or similes, whatever I'm doing here), or we'll be a Lincoln and Child — even better — churning permanent, excellent stuff out on a schedule. I don't know. And, though Paul and me are writing at a very similar level, I think, I'm finding we go about it completely differently. Paul writes like a novelist, I mean, which is a compliment. He actually pays attention to what came before, keeps in mind what's coming ahead. Unlike me. I just kind of jump in, figure I can get the continuity editor working later. Meaning, the way I do it's very inefficient, always dead-ends me a lot before I finally get to where I'm going. Which may of course happen to Paul as well, of course, but, the next piece of the story he sends me, anyway, it's always where it needs to be already, whereas I blast stuff back to him without having even reread it. So, I can't imagine I'm the ideal collaborator, but we're doing it anyway, and, more important, we're digging the story a lot. And, now — October for this — getting pretty close to a finished first draft. Also, it helps so much that Paul's agent, Stephen Barbara, knows the YA market so well. He's our Gandalf here.

What do you think would have happened without your freshman English teacher at Texas Tech? Do you think you would have been an English major and brought us this library of work?

Yeah, if I hadn't written that "The Gift" story for Dean Fontenont. Or, if she hadn't found it somehow, I forget exactly. Anyway, yeah, I mean, I came to school mostly to play, was one of those losers, had no plans on staying more than a year, was figuring I needed to be burning my good working years out on a tractor, making money, going to town on the weekends, but then I took this Reasoning course from this Philosophy TA "Biggs," I think it was — smart, smart guy — and, I don't know, it was like I saw how the world was put together. A real Terrence McKenna moment. So of course I hit Logic next, and it was so perfect, so wonderful, and I was completely planning on losing myself in Philosophy for the rest of my life, just sacrificing myself to it, but, at the same time, I was slowly becoming aware that the reason I was jamming at my Philosophy papers, it maybe wasn't that I was seeing all the way into Heidegger or Wittgenstein, it was that I could re-explain it all in my own language. Which is to say I could think, I could write. And argue, sure, but I'm not confident all that would have been enough, finally. So, yeah, I wound up having the campus police pull me from World Lit one day, spent three days and nights in the waiting room of the hospital, my uncle living or dying on the other side of those twin doors (living, still), and, because I had my World Lit spiral with me, and a pen I borrowed from somebody in the room, and time to kill, I wrote this story, "The Gift." Then, nine or so years later, my first novel hit the shelves. All makes perfect sense. How everybody does it, yeah? Yeah. But, I should say that, in fourth grade, I checked Where the Red Fern Grows out four times in a row — took me that long to get through it — and, at the end, that axe handle sticking in that tree, all rusted, a lantern hanging from it maybe, I distinctly remember thinking that I could do that, that I could stick that axe there, hang a lantern on it like that. So, writing, it was always kind of in my hip pocket, like a fallback. Which, that fallback, man, I used it a lot in high school, writing these long apology letters to different girls, leaving them under wiper blades, parking down the road until they'd had time to read them. That's writing in its most pure form, I think. The kind that gets you back in the door. True rhetoric there. Probably where I learned fiction.

I've noticed that you don't do a lot of big book tours. Is this a scheduling issue, or something else?

No, I dig getting out there, but usually it's via invited readings at different schools, institutions, libraries, book groups, all that. So, not so much a tour as scattershot stuff, just whenever, however. But, I do think that doing stuff on-line's coming to supplement, if not supplant, the old-fashioned book tour. However, if I could draw Palahniuk crowds, then I'd probably have no choice but to be out there. Very willingly.

For our writers out there, if you could have received one piece of advice, before you started writing, which you never got, what would it be?

Probably something one of my uncles told me, not about writing at all, but kids. He said that if you wait until you can afford it to have kids, then you'll never have kids. That's kind of how I've always gone about writing. No, I'm probably not talented enough or licensed enough or established enough to scrawl all over the spectrum like I do, or how I do, but no way's that going to stop me, either. I'm throwing darts at the dartboard, not from the other side of the room, but driveby, from a truck with bad tires, running a stop sign, the radio up just way too loud, in hopes everybody inside's going to look out, see me. And, I've got, what, eight or nine darts to stick so far? One of them's going to find the red, I know. Has to. Because I'm going to keep making that block, am not going to stop throwing.

You have two other books coming out in 2013 (Flushboy)

and 2014 (Not for Nothing), what can you tell us about these and is there anything else you're excited about?

Well, first, they're from Dzanc, which, how could I be more happy than to be working with them? They do quality stuff, are going to be even more important by 2013 and 2014. Very excited. And, these two, I guess I was already talking about them above, before I should have been, but Flushboy, it's finally a real and true love story, I think. About this kid kind of indentured by his entrepreneur dad into working the window at the family business, The Bladder Hut, a drive-through urinal. He kind of hates his job, hates his dad, hates his life, but it can all be saved, too, by one girl. It's exactly what being sixteen's like. To me anyway. And, Not For Nothing, man. So love this book. A second-person small-town noir, written about the same year I wrote Del Rio, I think. And, like Del Rio, it's set somewhere I used to live: Stanton, Texas. Only, I didn't just live in Stanton, I grew up there, it's still the place I consider home, the place I can still, for the Old Settlers parade, probably find my picture up in the drugstore window. And, the guy here, this excommunicated homicide detective, banished to living in a storage unit, all he wants is to drink himself into oblivion, maybe eat some pecan pie along the way. But people keep coming to him with cases, which, in good p.i. story fashion, all end up being the same case. Such a fun story, Not For Nothing. And Flushboy. I'll never not be in love with each of them.

As for what I'm excited about, though, that's easy: horror. This summer was The Passage — the vampire apocalypse starting up, here in the Denver area — right now Handling the Undead's doing stuff with zombies I haven't seen before, and there's Fringe on the TV, Supernatural, True Blood, and Scream 4's coming at us, and the Let Me In remake rocked . . . horror renaissance? Not quite. But that's just because horror's never really gone under. Horror's always been with us, it just seems more vital at certain times. Like, yeah, now, post 9/11, pre 2012.

We're going to look back on this as a vital decade for horror, I think. Not a Golden Age like the Eighties, I don't think, but there was so much excess in the Eighties that horror did let its own weight start to drag it down. Now, though, I think horror's leaner, meaner, more direct, has videogame injections and's just plain fun again, like it should be. I'm so glad to be a part of it. Or to be trying, anyway. No, no: I'm glad to be a consumer of horror right now, and hope that, in some way, I can give back to it.

How important is education in regards to your writing?

Completely important. You always hear that you're going to be the writer you're going to be, that all a writing program really does is accelerate the process, take twenty years down to three. And there's something to that. But, without grad school, first, I'd have never had William J. Cobb as my professor, and that, for me, meant everything. Reading him still, it's completely freaky, as I know the sentences and the rhythms so well. Just because I stole everything I could from him. And second, and only because it was second, I never would have worked with Janet Burroway, who taught me everything else. And not just about writing, but about being a writer. About living as a writer. Seriously, I fall back on her advice weekly, if not more. Without grad school, too, I don't know—I might have found Pynchon and Vizenor and John Barth and Percival Everett and Robert Coover. But I might not have, too. Not meaning at all to limit them to academia or anything. More like wondering what kind of writer I'd be if I hadn't encountered their writing, and been infected by it. Better, worse? No clue. Surely different. Which I guess is to say I don't believe that all a writing program does is speed up your development. It also changes who you are. And that ends up mattering.

What are three mistakes you made as a beginning writer?

Not picking a cooler name is definitely one. I mean, I could have gone with my Indian family name, but that felt cheap, as I'd never gone by it before, so it would look a lot like I needed to sell something, yeah? But still, 'Lovecraft,' 'King,' 'Cherie Priest,' 'ZZ Packer'—I'm always so completely jealous of names that are both real and cool. But I'm also jealous of ones that are cool and completely made-up. Too, as a kid, moving so much, I always got to change my name depending on where I was. But somehow I guess I thought that would never be over. Except now it is. I'm 'Stephen Graham Jones' forevermore. For a while, though, a few months in junior high, maybe, I was 'Stephen Presley.' I still want to be him. Though I had a perm then, and I don't want that again. And, the second mistake I guess I made was not lying enough on my cover letters. Of course I lied some, maybe even a lot, but why should the fiction only really start when you turn the page? And so what if you get caught? People respect a liar, I think. That's why they're into fiction. Third, I think third would be a mistake I made at Florida State University: Michael Jordan was playing in Atlanta, and I had a chance to go up, see him for the first and last time, and I didn't. I think about that a lot, now. I mean, I skipped a lot of AWPs and parties and bar meet-ups (I kind of hate bars) and coffeeshop hanging out (I despise the coffee) just so I could stay home, write a few more pages. And I know that's been the right decision, always. Anything that gets the words down on the page is always the right decision. But I keep thinking I could have written one story less, and maybe seen Michael Jordan play. I'd be a better person, I think.

Do you see publishing changing with all of the technological advances, today? How? Are you excited about it?

Yeah, very excited, but also very not worried about the physical technology of the book. I do think p-books are going to become more limited-type editions—or, the publishers are going to cue in that they need to not make them disposable, anyway, they need to make them to be a legitimate artifact, have cool endpapers, unique design, all that. People want to snort up book after book through their digital straws, right? I know I do. More more more, all of it, now. But I also want something to treasure.

And I don't want bookstores to go away. And I don't think they're going to, either. I mean, yeah, the chain bookstores are receding, which is changing the relationship of the publisher to the reader, but the industry will navigate. It has to, right? Not like the public's going to stop reading. People need stories like people need air. Engaging narrative is how we train ourselves to keep being ourselves—you learn how to tell your own story in your head, and how to edit it to fit. However, I am very interested in if e-books are some kind of midway point between p-books and the type of 'reading' experience in Stephenson's Diamond Age, say. Or Palahniuk's Rant. Those are technologies that are going to call for a completely different kind of writer. For stories that can't be bound between boards. I'm all for that happening, for storytelling to keep itself plugged in like that, to move along with the world instead of trying to act like an anchor, but it's kind of scary too, because I only know how to tell stories that a reader reads. Not one that the reader doesn't need words for. I'm willing to learn, though. Liars keep on lying, right? At work or at the bus stop, you're making stuff up. With or without words, I know I'll be lying. Except for here, to you, of course.

Thank you,
Goat

Bio

Stephen Graham Jones is the author of thirteen books. Most recent are Growing up Dead in Texas (MP Publishing) and Zombie Bake-Off (Lazy Fascist). Stephen's been a Stoker finalist, a Shirley Jackson Award finalist, a Colorado Book Award finalist, and has won an NEA and the Texas Institute of Letters Award for Fiction. Up next will be Flushboy and Not for Nothing (both Dzanc). Stephen's forty, married with children, got his PhD from Florida State University, and is a professor in the MFA program at the University of Colorado at Boulder. More at http://demon-theory.net

Vincent Louis Carrella

What comes to mind when you hear, "Mourning Goats?"

The world is a smoldering ash heap. Blackened oak silhouettes on bilge water horizons. There is no daylight and there is no moon. It is neither dark nor light. Everything is still and crackling. Miles and miles of hard pan flats rimmed by cinder cones. Spider web trails of ground-hugging soot. No wind. No ambient buzzing. And then there is the bell. A weak clatter, erratic in the heat waves. Some vague memory of green pastured dairyland, the vague sound of babies. The earth is bleating. The goats stand together, themselves blackened and shaggy like miniature Pleistocene oxen. A copper bell hangs from the neck of the big one, the leader. His horns are spirals of ancient wood. They bleat together sadly for the lost world.

You have one of the most beautifully written books I've ever read. It feels like you look at every word and perfect it. What is your process? Does it just flow like that or are you a master editor?

I close my eyes tightly and force myself to see. Sometimes I have to press the palms of my hands into my eyes so that the optic nerves are stimulated. I watch to see what happens. I can almost always see a place, and sometimes a person or parts of a person. I watch them to see what they do and I record that like a stenographer. Sometimes it comes easy but most of the time it doesn't. I struggle for every word and I think that it feels often like I build sentences out of bricks, one word at a time, hearing them together, and listening for an echo of resonance. I will often know the number of syllables for the word I am searching for before I find the word itself. I write words like I imagine a composer might write music. It's about cadences and feeling and sense. The poet Stanley Kunitz talks about this:

"The struggle is between incantation and sense. There's always a song lying under the surface of these poems. It's an incantation that wants to take over—it really doesn't need a language—all it needs is sounds. The sense has to struggle to assert itself, to mount the rhythm and become inseparable from it."

I relate to this idea of incantation and sense. When I heard this I identified with it and it helped me to affirm something I felt but could not articulate. I do a lot of revision and I read everything aloud all the time. It's always oral. It has to sound right to the ear and feel good moving through my mouth. With Serpent Box I wrote the whole thing long hand and then transferred it to the computer. I like to build things up over time, layer upon layer. I love the revision process. But I am a clumsy surgeon. I chop things up and splice things together like Dr. Frankenstein and then I smooth it all out, or I try to. I am far from a master of anything, let alone editing. I wish that it was like the old days and I had a trusty editor. Cutting things is awful. The first draft of Serpent Box was over 600 pages. I had to cut a lot of material I loved. But I did have an editor on that book. Her name is Marie Estrada. She was wonderful. I owe the whole thing to her, really. I lost her though. She left the business before the book came out and I have not spoken to her since nor have I given her a signed copy. I hope I can see her again before I die. If anybody knows where she is please tell her to get in touch with me.

Currently, you're the director of licensing at Nickelodeon Kids & Family Games Group and director of licensing at MTV Networks. When do you find time to write with such responsibilities? Do you find time?

I don't. I am hardly writing at all and it's taking its toll. I do write in the morning, but not for very long (I am writing this now in my precious few morning minutes). I am lucky if I get in an hour a day, which, if I'm lucky, is enough to complete a single paragraph. It's slow going. When I wrote the first draft of Serpent Box I was unemployed and married. I was very lucky that my wife supported me and the book. This is why I dedicated it to her. But all that has changed. I'm a part-time single father now and I must work a steady job. So time has become the biggest impediment to my work. Still, I squeeze it in. Right now, as I write this, I am sitting on a ferry making its way toward San Francisco just after dawn. This is a lovely way to work and I could see myself taking the trip back and forth for a few hours just to write. There is something about being close to the water that evokes images and emotion. Process changes. It evolves because I evolve. But I have only completed one novel so I don't think I'm really qualified to talk about process.

You have a pretty impressive background in video games. What are some of your favorite highlights from the gaming world?

I really enjoyed making games when I was part of a small team that had full creative control. We had a chance back in the 90's to create worlds that were visually compelling and also somewhat literate. At the time we were aiming for a new kind of story-telling, but after awhile I realized that the old kind of story-telling was really the most effective and most satisfying. Fiction gives the creator the most control. I was always a world builder in my own way. I used to play Dungeons and Dragons when I was a boy. But I soon grew tired of being among the hapless party of adventurers. I wanted to run my own dungeons. I wanted to build the worlds through which the other kids explored. When I became a dungeon master, that was the first time I remember feeling at home doing something. I have a clear memory of that feeling. Authoring an imaginary world that real people would willingly enter. Watching them and listening to them discover the fictional world of my creation. I don't get to do that anymore – watch people read my stories, but I do occasionally get a nice email or comment like the one you gave me, Goat. But if I had to pick a highlight from my gaming experience it would have to be when I was working on the CD-ROM game Bad Mojo. We came very close to something there. It was an immersive world, and a world that nobody had ever been to before. The world of a cockroach as seen through its eyes. And there was a story. A lousy story, but a story with real people and real lives, and the things you did in the roach-world had an effect on the human side of the story. The people who worked on that game were the best I've ever worked with and that was the pinnacle of my interactive gaming career. There are parts of me that want to do it again and as recently as yesterday I saw a compelling text-based 'game' experience on the web. I remember playing Multi-User Dungeon's, or MUDs, back in the early 90's. It was all user defined and on the fly, text only. There was something compelling about that idea that has yet to come to fruition. The potential for these new technologies to tell good stories has yet to be reached.

Who do you believe is the biggest influence of your work, up until now? Another author, friend, family member? Why?

I don't think it would be fair or honest to single out one person. I think Salinger was the first writer to reach me, but so many writers bled into my DNA. Jack London, Hemingway, Patrick O'Brian, even Stephen King. I was a huge Stephen King fan when I was young and I marveled at his ability to craft a believable world and to hold me there spellbound. But it took Cormac McCarthy to show me what was possible. Until I found his books I was drifting, What he showed me was a living model of what I was learning from John Gardner; which was a real example of how to spin a spell that holds the reader in the story, that sucks the reader into an utterly real and convincing world, and how to use words, language and sentence structure in that musical way I mentioned earlier. But it was more than that. McCarthy is a landscape writer and I am a landscape writer. This is a term I didn't discover until recently. It was brought to my attention by my dearest and best friend. For McCarthy the land itself is as much a character as any of his protagonists. Take The Road. That desolation was not devoid of character and menace. In every one of his books the land is part of the story. I realized through osmosis that whatever talent I may have springs from that same source. I am a product of the land. That is a strange thing to say from a boy from Long Island. But even Long Island has beauty and trees. We have big skies there too and we have torrential rain. We write so much about human interiors but I think it's more interesting to erase the boundary between outside and in. I can't speak for the masses. But for me, the land means something. Trees mean something. Sunlight affects me. A single cloud can make my day. So McCarthy gave me the confidence to write what I always felt about the natural world; which is a fickle character of both terror and beauty. There is no better character than the land around you.

Your mother and father divorced when you were five, but it sounds like your father showed you a true appreciation and love for nature. How do you think this shaped your life?

My father's insistence on being out in the woods was almost an obsession for him. I think it was the place he felt most comfortable, being, as he was, a policeman in a major city. But it also provided him with a free and easy way to entertain his sons. My father is a student of nature but he's also a consummate observer. He instilled in me the power of observation and an endless curiosity for the strange ways of nature. He knew the names of trees and animals and he was strict about the need for silence in the woods. He didn't only teach me to see, he taught me to listen. I fell in love with the woods as a boy at least partly because that's where I could be close to my father, but also because it tapped into my innate curiosity and urge to explore. The woods and the outdoors provided me with a feeling of safety and confidence – which I sorely lacked as a boy. I have turned to nature throughout my life for inspiration and for answers, but also for peace and solace. I think about the natural world much the same way I imagine an American Indian would. I respect it. It humbles me. I feel a certain spiritual harmony with it. But it also terrifies me. I had a recent experience in the wild that has altered my feelings about nature somewhat. I used to believe that in nature I was closer to God but now I am not so sure. God may have made the world but I am no longer convinced He manages it. The wild is just that – wild. And I don't always feel God there. I feel other things. Darker things. And that's all I want to say about that.

The way you talk of your childhood, insomnia, and where your mind went when you were alone, I would think that your writing would be much darker. How do you explain the crushing beauty that is Serpent Box?

I am flattered by your description, but I don't see much beauty in Serpent Box. I think it's a sad story with a lot of dark elements to it. I write dark things all the time, I just don't publish any of them. Serpent Box was my search for faith. It reflects a certain optimism I have in the world and for human beings. But the underlying current in that story is man's cruelty to man. What we do to other people who don't look like us or who threaten our view of life. We know that human beings are capable of horrific acts of violence, yet there is still love and light. I cannot reconcile this. I have my own beliefs about it that I won't get into here. But it's all there in the book, I think. And still those beliefs are evolving. Before Serpent Box I was not so sure about God so I asked 'Is there a God?' but now that point is clear and I am left with a question I keep coming back to. Who am I? I have always found light and I strive toward the light from the darkness. There are many things I choose not to write about because they are too dark. I choose to write with hope in my heart. I choose not to focus on death and violence. But I won't ignore those things either. I believe that for every act of evil or cruelty in this world there is an equal act of kindness and love. That's my philosophical equivalent to Newton's law. In Serpent Box I tried to include a lot of love because I think there's a balance and that in the end it all evens out. Though I hope that love does one day conquer all.

You once wrote one of my favorite lines about books, "Every great book is a funeral and a celebration." With this said, what do you think about the way we're getting our reading material these days, e-books, online, etc.?

Well, I believe in the book. I believe in the bound, physical, tactile experience of books. I believe that holding a book is a kind of magic. That carrying a book around, close to you, imparts a certain feeling. We spend so much time in front of screens. TV screens, movie screens computer screens. We are bombarded with digital data. We are addicted to electrons and tiny windows, and images. Why would we want to increase our exposure to electronic media? Are we not already over-exposed? Is there anybody out there who can make serious a case for more gadgets and devices? So-called "personal" electronics killed the vinyl album and those of us who are old enough to remember them miss them terribly. They gave us so much more to look at and learn about and feel from the musicians. And they were part of our physical space. Vinyl record albums occupied space in our lives. They were handled and touched. We had a relationship with the media that we no longer have. Do we really want to do this to books? All this technology is ostensibly about convenience, but do we really need to carry our entire record collections in our shirt pockets? Do we need all of our books all of the time? Is there not an art to selecting those few things we can carry with us? The tape we'll bring in the car? The book we'll choose for the plane? What happened to the joy of serendipity? Books are endowed with life. A human being writes them, a human being designs them and binds them and chooses the paper stock and typeface. There is something inherently missing in an e-book. What good is a soul without a body? We experience an actual book (an a-book) in three dimensions, but really we experience it in four. The fourth dimension is time. Right now I am carrying a copy of The Undiscovered Self by Carl Jung. It sat on my bedside table for a week before I chose to open it. I looked at it for a week. I saw it there from time to time as I was living my life. I read the spine and looked at Jung's face on the cover. I didn't know it but it was calling to me. Three days ago I picked it up and put it in the messenger bag I carry to work. It was with me for a few more days, just sitting in my bag where I was able to see it as I fished around for pens and papers. All the while it was speaking to me. Then I opened it and began to read it. I can quickly grab it from my bag whenever I have a few spare moments, whenever I am waiting for a bus or a ferry. When I have to move quickly I can jam it back in. As I am reading it I take out a pencil to make notes in the margins or use a highlighter to mark a phrase I want to come back to. I can bend the corners of the pages if I want to mark them for future reference. This book is with me during a certain time of my life. It will only be with me for a week or so. This weekend I will bring it on the plane when I go to L.A.. This book, and this book alone, will be my companion during the month of October 2010. I will mark the date on the inside cover. In this way this book, an a-book, becomes part of me and part of time. It is unique. Its size, its shape, its cover, its typeface, its pages. It is not some homogenized experience. So there is no case to be made for e-books. The e-book is a scam, a fraud, a great tragedy. They were invented to make corporations more money, not for our comfort and convenience. It's planned obsolescence. Buy more. Consume more. Milk more money from intellectual property. I refute, rebuke and reject them. To me they are the equivalent of the Real Doll, the surrogate artificial lover. An e-book will never whisper. An e-book will never put out a subtle call from the shelf, or jump out at me from time to time after I've read it, enticing me to pick it up again. Book lovers understand what it feels like to be in a roomful of books, to be surrounded by them. A-books, real books, are endowed with the spirits of those who made them and that is not something an e-book can ever do. This is a sort of genocide in my opinion. And we are all complicit in this eradication of something beautiful and yes, klunky, heavy, awkward to hold. But so what? We should be willing to bear the weight of something that we are willing to make a part of us.

I heard there was a short story collection in the works, is there any truth to this? Is there anything you can tell us about this, or your current project?

I have been writing short stories since I finished Serpent Box and have what amounts to a collection, but I am not yet sure it stands together as a unified whole. I put them all together recently and thought I had something interesting and unique. But time spoiled that. After letting them sit for a couple months I went back to them and re-read them and lost faith. So now I'm not so sure. I've decided that they are not good enough yet, they need a lot more work, so what I'm considering now is whether or not I want to invest the time it will take to not only revise what I have but to write some more. It's as much work as a novel and I'm thinking maybe I should just write a novel but I am having problems with that as well. I have not been able to arrive at a decision as to which of several ideas to write about. I seem to change my mind every other day. I have two or three things I am passionate about but I don't want to elaborate on them. Hemingway said that talking about a story in progress is like rubbing the dust off a butterfly's wings. So I'm going to keep the butterflies to myself for now.

On your website, you have letters that you wrote about how Serpent Box came together, where you were at in the book, and your inner-workings. Do you think this kind of freedom to put these out for all to read disappeared after the book was published? Are you still writing these letters, to Andrew, today?

I read this question, I felt the urge to cry. No, I am not writing the letters to Andrew today and maybe that's part of my problem. Andrew L. Wilson is a brilliant writer and he was my mentor. He gave generously of his wisdom and his time during my darkest hours. He loved me unconditionally and he loved my writing. I could not have written Serpent Box without him. During the past few years we've become estranged and I regret that. I could sure use him right now, and maybe that's why I feel so uncomfortable. I don't want to 'use' him that way without being able to give back and I don't know that I have anything to give. He wrote a novel that really moved me and gave me the courage to write from my heart. It's still one of the best books I've ever read and yet it's not been published because the book business is so brutal and cruel. But maybe I will write to Andrew again. I used to write to him without expecting a response and he answered maybe 1 out of 10 of my letters; which was okay by me. I didn't always need him to respond, I just needed him to be there, because writing is so damn lonely and depressing sometimes. Writers need each other. I know I do. I need other people around me who are reaching for something beyond themselves and trying to find some meaning in this life. Andrew was instrumental in the formation of the final version of Serpent Box. You should interview him.

You say that you were not trained as a writer but you learned how to write by reading. What books were your biggest influences?

I've mentioned that Cormac McCarthy's sensibilities and use of language appeal a great deal to me. He creates the most compelling landscapes – both physical and psychological – of any writer I've read. All the Pretty Horses was my entrée into McCarthy and I think it was a great place to begin. But Blood Meridian also captured my imagination and, to this day, is the most powerful novel I've read. But my favorite McCarthy book is The Crossing, which is the second book in the border trilogy. Like McCarthy, I am also interested in the transition of boys into men.

He sees through a different lens of course being of an older generation but at the core I deeply understand his younger characters. I would also say that Call of the Wild was a book that proved instrumental in my thinking and development as a writer. London is also a landscape writer, as is Hemingway. I came to Hemingway late in life. I had always avoided him because I felt that he was too obvious and too popular. I intentionally ignored him because I didn't want to be influenced by him. The same is true for Faulkner. When I read The Old Man and the Sea however, I understood that I had been missing something that could have helped shaped me as a human being, forget about being inspired as a writer. I looked down my nose at all those books that we were compelled to read in high school, since I was rebellious and anti-establishment as a boy. But that was foolish of me and arrogant. When I look back on it books like Catcher in the Rye, A Separate Peace, Slaughterhouse Five, Siddartha, 1984, Of Mice and Men, Lord of the Flies and Salinger's Nine Stories were the very bedrock foundation of my literary soul. Thank you English teachers, everywhere, my writing, the fact that I write at all, I owe to you, Mr. Broza, Mr. Gober, Mrs. Dissen.

You once said, "I think I am trying to convince myself that I am sane." This goes through my head often when I write, maybe writing is the only thing that keeps me sane, do you want to go delve deeper into this thought? You wrote that line eight years ago, what does it mean to you now?

It means more to me now than it ever has before, because I am basically a neurotic who cannot stop thinking, cannot stop the words and images and emotions and ideas from making themselves heard. I write because I don't know what it means to be alive. And I don't understand why God made the world, or why He made man this way – so fallible. I don't understand the behaviors of human beings. Life is a mind-boggling mystery to me and writing helps me to gain just a little bit of insight into what it means to be living and to make some sense of it all. I have said that writing is organized thinking - thought recorded and carefully arranged to create an emotional and intellectual effect. So the mere act of sculpting thoughts, observations and ideas into a cohesive whole helps me to understand the world and to understand myself. I don't know why it is so, but I know that when I am writing, steadily, I am much less edgy and prone to depression. Writing helps me to organize what I'm feeling but it does much more than that, because journaling accomplishes this same thing. To be clear I am talking about writing stories, fiction, and I am only talking about my own experiences. Writing is very personal and precious. To tap into my subconscious is to tap into the collective subconscious of the world. Thus, when I am writing, as Salinger would say "with all my stars out", I am communing with mankind, all the living and all the dead. That's how I see it. Stories are floating through the air like radio waves. Radio waves that are millions of years old are bombarding the earth from other galaxies. I don't want to get too metaphysical here but there is so much we don't know, don't see. Read about string theory and it'll blow your mind. Alternate planes of existence? Parallel universes? I already know there's a spirit world. So it makes sense to me that there's this stream of stuff floating around, the collective experience of man. Archetypes. Funny I'm reading Jung again now. I am fascinated with the collective subconscious. Maybe the voices I hear and the things that I feel are echoes of that. I don't know. I just know that I feel at home when I'm writing. It feels natural to me and most of the time it feels good.

You turned a twelve page short story into a novel, how does this happen? Did you know you were writing a novel when you started?

I started Serpent Box as a short story. I had no intention of writing a novel. But the story garnered some attention when it won the Literal Latte Fiction Award in the year 2000. At the time

I was 35 years old but I was a very young writer and all I wanted to do was write some good short stories and work my way up to a novel by the time I was 45. I gave myself 10 years. But an agent saw the story and she convinced me to turn it into a novel. I did that bit by bit. 50 pages here, 20 pages there. I didn't think I could write a novel. But this story dovetails into your question 19 so why don't I leave it at that and get into there?

What is/was your daily writing routine like? Do you have one?

You ask two questions here. What was my routine like (I assume during Serpent Box) and do I have one now? During Serpent Box I would write every morning from about 8:30am until noon or 1. I'd go to a local café and write in long-hand. I'd do each chapter in long-hand and then transcribe it to the computer. I think I filled 26 notebooks. I would often read a bit before I got started or write a letter. I wrote to Andrew Wilson as a way of warming up and preparing myself for the day's work ahead. I borrowed that idea from John Steinbeck who wrote a daily letter to his editor Pascal Cavici while working on East of Eden. I thought this was a fine idea and it wound up working very well for me. In this way I would organize my thoughts and pin down what problems I was facing on that given day. What will Jacob do now that Charles is dead? How will Rebecca get to Georgia? Should I bring Hosea Lee into the story so late?

My routine today is much less organized. I don't have the luxury of unemployment and my days are not my own. I have to squeeze my writing in when I can. Usually I will write on the thirty minute ferry ride between Marin and San Francisco. An hour is not much but it's enough to keep a story going. I've written several stories this way. I am a morning person and have a difficult time writing at night. I wish I was one of those night owl writers, but I can't focus at all after dark. I do think a ritual and a routine is important, at least for me, so maybe that's something I should look into starting again.

We hear all the time that one should "write what they know," if this is true, how did Serpent Box come to be? Did you do a lot of research or was this something you were familiar with?

I have a big problem with "write what you know", because I think it is misinterpreted. I don't think it necessarily means write about your life as a mailman or theme your story on your background in plumbing. Though any of those could be fascinating in the hands of a good writer. While your background and experience can add a lot to your writing, I take "write what you know" to mean what you know in your heart. What do you believe is true and valuable? I know the world can be cruel and unjust, but I also know it is capable of beauty and grace. That's my truth. That's what I know.

But for me, I have a different aphorism I live by: Write what you don't know. I knew nothing about the rural south. I know nothing about Holiness Pentecostals, or snake-handling, or God. I knew little of what it meant to have so much faith, so much conviction. But I wanted to know these things. Why did these people risk their lives drinking poison? Why do they believe so fervently in the Gospel of Mark? What does the bible really mean? These were questions I needed to answer for myself. So I just read the bible, and I read biblical analysis, and I read first-person accounts about what it's like to handle serpents, and I read about the Holiness movement and I read about rural Tennessee and Georgia and Appalachian Folklore and I read about the terrible legacy of lynching in America. I looked at old photos and watched some documentaries and then I sat down and wrote. I wouldn't say I did a lot of research. I did just enough to infuse myself with a spirit and the rest I made up. I didn't want the book to be accurate, I wanted it to be mythical and rich with feeling. I wanted it to feel like a dream. Dreams contain both concrete truths and ephemeral possibilities. That's what I did, I recorded my dream.

There's a quote, "I read so I can live more than one life in more than one place," by Ann Tyler, do you believe that authors live more than one life as a result of their stories?

I can't speak for all authors. I don't know what they feel or experience. I don't talk to a lot of writers. I know that for me it's not about living more than one life, it's about projecting myself through a prism so that I can see all my component colors. I don't need to write to feel like I live more than one life. I feel like I've already lived a dozen, which may be one of the reasons why I am so compelled to write, or why my head is so full of vivid images that surely don't come from this life I'm living now. This jibes with what I was saying earlier. The characters and places I write about don't feel strange to me. I am not visiting them, I am liberating them. I feel like they're already inside me. But as a reader, now that's a different story. I am a reader first, and I became one in order to escape. So Ann Tyler's quote holds true for me, as a reader. Yet even those people, other author's characters, when written well, they feel like they are mine too. Sometimes though it is purely vicarious. Take Shantaram. What an incredible journey that was. What an amazing book. I can't relate to any of those characters but I sure didn't mind going for that 600 page ride.

I've noticed that you're a fantastic photographer; do you think there's any correlation between the way a writer sees the world and the way everyone else sees it?

I love this question and I thank you for the kind words about my photography. It has always been a passion of mine. I began taking pictures long before I began to write. I think that many writers see deeply, beyond the mere surfaces of things and some writers are like photographers of the soul. I think Don DeLillo is one of those. He has an eye that is just uncanny. He notices every detail of even the most mundane thing and he shows it to us as something not at all mundane. Again, I don't know how anyone else sees the world. I imagine that writers and photographers and painters and police detectives see it more closely. My father was a policeman and he taught me to look at things closely and to examine everything. He taught me pattern recognition and how to spot things that didn't belong in a given scene. So from boyhood I was trained to look, though I think it came naturally to me since I've always had this ability to find things – watches, money, jewelry. I was born with, as my father would always say, a good game eye. My mother was a photographer and painter and she taught me how to use a 35mm SLR. Photography was very important in our home. The captured image was always something that intrigued me. Photography allows me to save precious moments and to chronicle what I find interesting. It also serves my collector nature. I collect things, physical objects, but I also collect memories. I suppose this is rooted in a fear of losing memory, or of losing time. When I write I often write about memory. Perhaps this is the correlation you're looking for. I write stories that focus on memories and things that evoke memories. A good writer is like a photographer I think. She composes a photograph of an event, or captures a frozen moment in time and renders it to the reader as a clear image, or series of moving images. But a whereas a photographer aims the lens outward, at the external world, the writer aims his lens inward where the picture is not so clear. But you asked me if I saw a correlation between the way a writer sees the world and the way everyone else sees it. What you're really asking is if there's a correlation between how an artist sees the world and how "everyone else" sees it. But I would ask is there really an everyone else? And what is the difference between a person who chooses to express her interpretation of life and the world and a person who does not? What does it mean to be a creator of art? What is art? Why do some of us need to do it while others do not? And, more importantly to me, would we all, given the right encouragement and opportunity, be artists of some kind or another? Is art, and the creative drive, latent in us all? I think it is, to a degree. But how we process what we see, how if effects us and then what we do with those feelings and ideas evoked by our senses, that's what makes a poet or a sculptor and not a toll collector or a politician.

If you could go back ten years and give yourself one piece of advice, what would it be?

There are so many things I would advise my younger self to change or avoid, but I think one thing I would counsel that young writer to do would be to not focus at all on publication and to not get caught up in the machine of the publishing business. Just write. Write what you want and expect nothing. Be more judicious with your time. Read more. Experiment more. I think that I have gotten sidetracked by things like book marketing and blogs when I should have been writing. I read that Michangelo's last words were "Draw Antonio, draw. While there is still time." Antonio was his assistant and he was telling him to just do the work, just do that thing that drove you to create in the first place. Time is so precious. We're here to write, not Tweet or blog.

Do you think Serpent Box would have ever come to fruition without the push of Lane Zachary? Could you tell us about that?

It would never have come to fruition as a novel without Lane. She saw something in me, and in that story that I didn't see and she pulled it out of me like a stubborn tooth. She took me under her wing and gave me the encouragement I needed to write the book. I would write a little at a time and then show her the results and she would tell me it was good and urge me to write more. While she never guaranteed me publication she did guarantee me serious consideration. I know that if I finished a decent draft of the book that it would be seen and have a shot. But as important as Lane was, Serpent Box owes its existence to many people, all of whom I mention in my acknowledgements. Marie Estrada was a key contributor and champion and Laura Strachan was absolutely critical and in many ways more important than even Lane in that she responded to me during that very dark and difficult time when I was hunting for a new agent. She got the book out there. She got it in front of Marie. So many people are a part of Serpent Box that I feel that singling out one of them is unfair. Terry MacMillan....

I feel like you found out a lot about yourself when you toured for Grateful Dead, can you tell us a little bit about what came out of that cross-country tour?

You're talking about the summer of 1988 when I left New York for California. I think that was *the* defining moment of my life. I needed to break away from everything I knew, and everything I was comfortable with in order to begin to discover who I am. I lived in a constant state of fear and dread in New York and I lacked the courage to be my authentic self. I spent over a month on the road with my two best friends selling tee-shirts at Dead shows in order to eat and buy gasoline. I learned a lot that summer, but the journey is not over. In many ways I am still on that trip, I am still learning who I am. What the Grateful Dead teaches me, through their lyrics and philosophy, is that everything's going to be alright. Don't worry so much. Life is a cyclic escalation of joys and plummets into sadness. They remind me to be happy with what I have and to be grateful for it. They remind me that there is a lesson in everything and an answer where you least expect it. They are really an optimistic band. They're all about hope in the midst of madness and despair. They are about resurrection and redemption. Even their name suggests this. Legend has it that Phil Lesh chose that name at random out of a dictionary of myths and legends. I found that dictionary and I own two copies. The funny thing is that book has led me in all different directions. I've used it in my own work time and time again. The Dead are all about these connections, and serendipity, and light at the end of the tunnel. They are also about paying attention and observation. Robert Hunter and John Perry Barlow are overlooked in the pantheon of great lyricists. As much as I love Jerry Garica and Bob Weir and Phil Lesh (and of course Mickey and Bill and PigPen and Keith and Brent) it is Barlow and Hunter I admire most and who keep me connected to the music. They are great poets whose words are as much part of me as Rumi and Whitman. I listen to the Grateful Dead for the music, but they stay in my heart because of the words. Just keep moving, don't give up, tomorrow is another day, look on the bright side, sometimes you win and sometimes you lose, love conquers all, don't worry be happy. You hang out with these old hippies and the hardcore followers that call themselves the family and you see that these people didn't have a pot to piss in. They lived one day at a time and there was an odd Zen quality to them. People often disparage hippies but hippies are optimists and humanitarians.

How important is your education in regards to your writing?

I'm not sure how to answer this question. If what you mean is my overall education, the formal education that spanned my early childhood and young adulthood, then I would say that it has been vitally important. Crucial in fact. The early and persistent habit of reading and then writing is what has given me the raw source of inspiration I draw from. The foundation of story-telling and mythology and science that I was raised on all came out of schools and out of books. Teachers have also been vital to my thinking. They have liberated me from the little prisons of ignorance, stubbornness and judgment I was trapped in.

But if you're asking about my writing education, then my answer would be different because I have not received any. Not formally. On that front the best education for me has been a voracious reading habit and a sacred love of books, real books, made from pulped tree corpses and ink. I try to read great books and pay close attention to how they are constructed. But I'm a self-taught writer with no MFA.

How do you know when a book is "finished?"

I suppose it depends on what you mean by the word 'finished'. Because there are, I think, several finish lines that one crosses when working on a novel. There is the finish line you get to when you've completed the first full draft of the manuscript and the finish of handing off the revised draft to an agent or editor and then there's the finished of seeing the book in galley form when you know it's then only a matter of grammatical polish. And then, there is the finished of seeing the book on a shelf. Each of those milestones is big but none of them is final. Not even the book sitting on the shelf.

I've only written the one novel so I don't think I have a handle yet on what it feels like to know that I'm finished. But with Serpent Box, when I finally saw the climax and then trusted it enough to go with it, I knew I was 'done'. It was just a matter of writing it down. But done done? There was a feeling. It was an intuitive moment, just as there are so many intuitive moments in my writing and I think for a lot of writers. Sometimes you just know. It's a feeling, like the one you get before a lucky streak, or when you're in the ocean and you know you need to get out of the water.

But it's also not that simple. At least it wasn't for me. Because Serpent Box sat for months 'unfinished' even after the whole story was down on paper. Something was missing from the story. Its structure was not right and Lane Zachary, my agent at the time, saw that. So I spent a week on the coast of Maine with my good friend and fellow writer Andrew Wilson, who advised me in a major re-structure of the narrative. But even then the book was not 'finished'. Because after my current agent Laura Strachan brought the book to Harper-Collins my editor there, Marie Estrada made several recommendations to me that forced me to re-examine the story - again! I went back and wrote an entirely new opening chapter and made some significant tweaks to parts of the book. So finished is subjective. And it's a word I'm going to be a lot more careful about using in the future.

What are your thoughts on basing your characters on real people?

All my characters are real people. I believe that. They come to me from the dead. I really don't know how else to explain it because I can literally see them and hear them speak, so they are very real to me. But I think the question means real as in real human beings we know from our lives and experiences. I have never done this, not consciously. And I don't think I would do it. I might, but so far I haven't felt the desire or necessity to use people I have known as inspirations for characters.

What are three mistakes you made as a beginning writer?

Not having enough faith in the revision process, in my own judgment and in my intuition. I think that's the first mistake I made. Thinking that I can only write well under certain circumstances or under certain conditions. That was another. But I made so many, and still do. I still consider myself a beginning writer.

But I've made many mistakes, including comparing myself to other writers or worrying about other writers and their success/lack of success. Worrying about getting published. Thinking things will get easier once I was published. Worrying about marketing my work. Worrying about my name or my 'career'. Thinking that research will solve a problem/relying too much on research. Worrying about a plot and/or thinking about a plot. Thinking too much about what a story should be. Using too much dialog. Using too much exposition. Not trusting the readers' intelligence enough. Listening to critics. Letting people who don't understand my work read my work. Telling people too much about what I was doing. Pushing a story too hard too fast (not giving it the time to develop naturally if it needs to). Waiting too long to kill my darlings (to cut what I liked reading when it didn't serve the story). Underestimating how hard it is to write something I can be proud of. That's more than three but never let it be said I don't give you your money's worth.

Do you have a favorite part about being a published writer?

Hands down my favorite thing about being a published writer is being granted the occasional privilege of reading my work aloud to other people and to connect with readers. It's especially humbling to hear a reader tell you that he or she was moved by my book or that they really liked a certain part. It's nothing short of miraculous to share something that was once in my mind with another person who seems to get it. If I had my druthers I'd be on tour constantly, reading in small bookshops and talking to readers.

Do you see publishing changing with all of the techno-logical advances, today? How? Are you excited about it?

Heavy sigh. I *do* see publishing changing, but I honestly cannot say I understand it. I don't know much about how the publishing business works in the first place, so it's hard to talk about how it has changed or what it might become. I know that digital publishing and eBooks have become this huge force of nature that seems impossible to ignore. When I think about it, I'm not even sure my next novel will make it into traditional print, which is depressing to me. Because I love the physical medium and believe that it has value far, far beyond mere nostalgia. For me, a great book speaks. I'm talking about the physical incar-nation of a book, bound in paper. A book on a shelf, or on a table or even in a person's hands has a voice that a collection of zeroes and ones contained within a jpeg cover image simply does not. Digital publishing flattens and homogenizes books. Trapped within tablets and devices they are hidden from view. They become two-dimensional. They become reduced to miniature images, lines of text, that only the bearer of the device can see, and even then only if he or she actively chooses to look for them. And that word, actively, is really the crux of my concern. Because so many books that have made a big difference in my life were books that I did not actively seek out, but were books that spoke to me from a shelf, or from the hands of some stranger holding it on a bus.

I am not excited by today's 'advances' in publishing. I am saddened by them. I see the extinction of the tangible book on the horizon. I see the end of print. I don't see technological advances in terms of storage, distribution and playback to be a good thing. We are losing something vital when we can no longer hold a book in our hands and when it no longer stands out as a distinct entity that exists in the three-dimensional space of our lives.

Thank you,
Goat

Bio

Vincent Louis Carrella is a father, writer and photographer who lives in Marin County, CA. He escaped New York in the late 1980's to follow the Grateful Dead in a Dodge van and ran out of money in San Francisco. He is the author of Serpent Box (Harper/Perennial) a novel about a snake-handling Holiness boy born deformed within a hollow lynching tree Depression era Tennessee. His stories, poetry and essays have appeared in Stone Voices, Warmed & Bound, Linnaean St.com, Literal Latte, Talking Kitchen, See You Next Tuesday and BoundOff.

Craig Clevenger

What comes to mind when you hear, "Mourning Goats?"

I've never heard a mourning goat, so I don't know. If I have, I didn't know they were in mourning.

"Mourning" hits me as a verb in this case, so it sounds like a band. Like "Flogging Molly," maybe. But definitely the act of mourning , some person or persons are mourning their deceased goats. So what makes these goats so significant? What kind of people hold goats in such high regard? Maybe they're a tribe of itinerant herders, and that all their goats are dead means there's some maurading predator that's begun to wreak havoc on their way of life. Questions come to mind, which make for stories.

As an author, what do you think taught you the most about writing, and why? Education? Experience? Writing?

Reading and writing. Reading always came first. And I then learned by doing, by writing, making mistakes and learning from them, and ultimately cultivating a regular writing habit. College writing workshops were a major part of my education, but the ceiling for what you can learn from workshops is lower than most people think. Workshops get you out of your own head, and they teach you to see your work from a cold perspective.

But there comes a point where you realize you could run yourself ragged trying to account for all of the criticism that comes your way. You could transcribe Nabokov and pass it through a workshop and it's going to bleed red ink from all the feedback. It's important to gain what you can from the input, but it's equally important to know when criticisms are made just for the sake of speaking up in class. When you can identify that point—when the criticism ceases to be helpful—you're done.

Experience is important, but it's a mistake to think a writer needs to actively seek or have some kind of adventure to write about. Birth, death, falling in love, etc., happen in the blandest parts of suburbia or remote countryside as much as anywhere else. Observation is critical; without it, experience is meaningless.

When Dermaphoria came out, you said that you thought you would lose some fans because it's completely different than your first novel, The Contortionist's Handbook, while I don't believe this was the case, what are your thoughts on your current project?

The current project is a big change of direction for me. It's not a neo-noir novel like my first two.One reader described an early chapter as magical-realist, but that chapter is from one of three distinct story threads, so it's not a reflection of the entire book. Two of those story threads are written in the third person, whereas my first two novels were both entirely first-person narratives.

I want to be a different writer with each book. I'm not interested in "pushing the envelope" or being "transgressive." But I do want each book I write to exceed the previous one. While I'd like to have a steady but growing audience, I don't want to write the same thing, or in the same style, over and over.

Bolivia, what's the best story that came out of your stay there (not fiction)? What was it like living with author, Wendy Dale?

What few stories I do have are on my web site. I called the travel diary "Dispatches from Interzone," but it's only three or four entries. I didn't get out much except for groceries or coffee. The whole point of going to Bolivia was so I could stretch out my last royalty payment. My Spanish is crude, at best; I had no wifi in the house; the dvd player on my laptop was busted; I only knew Wendy and her boyfriend; I was in a virtual writing lockdown for three months, and it was the most productive I've been in years. Living with Wendy Dale was cool. She's a night owl, just like me. And she's extremely hard working with her writing. We rarely interacted, except for once a week at the kitchen table where we'd shoot the shit into the wee hours with her boyfriend. The three of us called the place, La Casa Vampiro.

You've done a few classes over at the Cult, have you thought of taking teaching further? Have you been approached?

When the Cult first offered me a teaching gig, I was reluctant. I'm always learning, and didn't think I had anything to add to the existing repertoire of creative writing "how to" books, classes and web sites.

The classes have been a success, overall. I just wrapped up my latest one, and I've got a standing offer to teach again. We'll see.

In the past you described your writing process as, "going in the pit," does this happen with every piece you work on? Was it different with your new piece?

"The Pit." That's my colorful way of saying I have a dedicated place to work, and I tune out distractions, turn off my phone and email. Ideally, anyway. It's been tougher with this new one. Aside from my time in Bolivia, I've seldom had a dedicated space to work on this new one. The last few years since "Dermaphoria" have been up and down. I've moved several times. Lots of couch-surfing, and the lack of stability makes it hard to get lost in a writing project.

The last interview I read of yours, it said that you were looking for an agent, have you found one yet?

Not yet. I've had a few inquiries about the synopsis and sample chapters, but I'm still working on this rewrite, so nobody's seen the finished manuscript.

With your new book, you holed up in a hotel with Chris Baer (Will Christopher Baer) at the beginning; do you still share your writing with him? Are there any plans for another meeting with the windows blacked out?

Chris and I have talked on and off about doing a screenplay together, either feature-length or some sort of serialized tv-drama. Aside from that, we correspond semi-regularly—a one or two-week email volley every five or six months—but otherwise never talk writing. We'll convene again at some point in our virtual fallout shelter with a big-ass whiteboard, our laptops, a library and a coffee maker. No telling what we'll emerge with or how long it'll take.

You have one of the coolest tattoos I've ever seen, the Sisyphus tattoo. What others do you have that you want to share? What do they mean to you?

They all mean different things. Among the more significant is the six-fingered handprint I had tattooed on my left wrist after I completed a draft of my first novel. I haven't had any since then, except for a little color or detail added here and there. It's been several years since I've had enough cash to indulge in more ink, but I am by no means finished. My left sleeve is more or less done; my right is still empty below the elbow.

The Sisyphus tattoo you mentioned, it's a reminder of the daily office grind I'd been at for fifteen years or so that I gave up to pursue writing. It gives me some perspective when I think about the money I could have accumulated in the last ten years, had I stayed in the business world. I have a heart on my inner-left forearm; it's anatomically realistic, but it's been sutured together. It followed a rough period years back, and it's an illustration of putting my life back together. Then there's the traditional Virgin of Guadalupe on my right shoulder, but instead of the Virgin Mary icon, it's Alice from the original woodcut illustrations of "Alice in Wonderland." The closest thing I have to any real ethnic identity is my Catholic upbringing, so I wanted to acknowledge that. But being a fallen non-believer, replacing the image with a fairy tale more accurately reflected my beliefs.

How much research goes into your books? I know that you read through psychiatric books and art forgery books for The Contortionist's Handbook and Dermaphoria, what kind of books are you looking into for Saint Heretic?

It's unlikely that "Saint Heretic" will remain the title of this one, for a number of reasons. We'll see. Anyway, the nature of the

Handbook's narrator, John Vincent, required the story to be laden with the minutiae of his criminal life. I wrote it to sound like someone talking to themselves while seriously coked-up, so the recitation of trivia was part of the voice. But I'm doing less and less research as time goes on, because I want to engage the reader with the story instead of hooking them with random factoids. Looking back, I would have written that book very, very differently.

With "Dermaphoria," some research was of course necessary, but I wasn't interested in tittlating readers with a how-to on crystal meth or LSD manufacture. More importantly, the story wasn't about drugs, it was about human touch, connection and identity.

And now there's this third novel, maybe "Saint Heretic," maybe not. There's no criminal enterprise in this one, as with the first two. It's all just things happening, the characters and what they say and do.

Ultimately, I enjoy the analogue outlining process more than the research. Like having a map of the Mojave Desert on my wall when I wrote DpH, with photographs from a road trip tacked around it. Or sometimes I'll find a magazine picture of someone who matches my mental image of a character and I'll clip that out. Or spreading out pages from blank calendars to mark events in the story, to make certain there aren't any misfires in chronology between the backstory and present narrative, or that I'm correctly citing an event from a character's past. I love letting the process take up physical space around me, as long as I've got a dedicated work space. It lets me physically immerse myself in the story as well as mentally.

I just read your short story, Mercury, on my kindle, what do you think about e-books? Good/Bad/Indifferent?

I don't know where to begin with this one. I've committed to writing a piece about my whole take on e-books and the future of publishing (this stemmed from my last writing class, after a similar question from one of my students). I don't think they're good or bad; they're simply the next wave. I can think of a score of practical uses for an e-reader, such as for traveling or if I were a law student. But I love books. I love paper and ink and binding and holding one in my hands. I like the artifact of the thing, the way it soaks up its own history as it gets shelfworn, re-read, lost, stolen, sold, lent out and damaged. I love the saying, "a room without books is like a body without a soul."

I don't have an opinion about e-books as much as I have an opinion about the starry-eyed incredulity of the publishing industry toward the advent of e-books. I started to write a more detailed response to this, and I stopped myself when it hit the four-page mark.

You seem to almost play games with your books, like when John Dolan Vincent visited in Dermaphoria, are there plans to keep these visits going?

Dermaphoria's narrator, Eric Ashworth, is seriously paranoid. His pattern recognition filters have been blown wide open, so he sees signals, messages and threats everywhere. The story reflects that, in its own set of cues and signals buried within the text. Eric is convinced the chirping crickets he hears at night are transmitting signals and ratting him out. If you follow the Morse code as relayed by Eric in the narrative, the dots and dashes of the chirping crickets spell out "chirp, chirp, chirp." Part of that was meant to layer the novel, to have all of these hidden things be discoveries the reader makes with subsequent readings. The crickets chirping, the dog barking, the bug bites on his arms, the names of characters and code names for labs, all of these are pieces of Eric's paranoia manifested in the story. The appearance of John Vincent was part of that, yes, but also a way of playing a game, of nodding to readers of the first book, to see if they could catch that. And to be honest, after narrating a whole novel from Vincent's point of view, it was fun describing him from the outside, as a total stranger. Yeah, he'll be back in the third novel.

Maybe.

Someday I want to do an entire novel like this, a single block of narrative game-playing like Calvino's "If On A Winter's Night A Traveler" or "The Castle of Crossed Destinies." I have lots of ideas for the kinds of games I'd like to play, but they all have to take a back seat to character and story.

If I remember right, wasn't Wendy Dale a big part of jumpstarting your career? What went down?

Wendy Dale is responsible for Chuck Palahniuk reading my first novel. Actually, Dennis Widmyer, the webmaster for chuck-palahniuk.net, passed it onto Palahniuk, but Wendy sent it to Dennis. We'd never even met, she just thought the book deserved some exposure. We corresponded after that, met a few times while she was living in L.A., the first time was during Palahniuk's "Diary" tour, and we've kept in touch ever since. But with Wendy getting it to Palahniuk, yeah, things got a jumpstart. More than just an Amazon spike while he was touring, he gave me a slow-burn longevity. And given how unprolific I am, slow burn is a good thing. Indeed, I owe Wendy Dale, bigtime. So on that note, everyone, buy her book, "Avoiding Prison and Other Noble Vacation Goals."

You've had a lot of different jobs since your first book, are you still working in the bars or are you doing something else? How does that affect your writing?

Most of my jobs have been bar tending, with one stint working at a bookstore, plus the occasional teaching gig. The jobs don't really affect my writing, but they're good for my mental health. Too many days with the windows blocked out, staring at a notebook and talking to sock puppets…that's not good for my sanity. Bar tending keeps me in touch with humanity. The trick is, as every writer knows, to balance the necessity of work while carving out time to write. Which I'm not doing right now. I've pushed everything aside so I can finish this re-write and start circulating this manuscript.

Now that you're stateside, what's a day in the life of Craig, look like?

I haven't had a typical day in months. I've moved twice since I got back, so haven't been able to establish a routine. I just finished putting my library back into storage, and I'm living on a friend's couch right now. The dust is settling and I'm pulling out of my funk; I've been hitting the gym in my friend's condo complex and indulging in the odd vegetable or two. I shrank down to "The Machinist" level of weight while in Bolivia, and putting the pounds back on has been a bitch. But I'm eating and exercising, and the hard work of moving is done, at least for now. I got some recent feedback on the first chapters of the novel, and I've returned to it in earnest. My ideal routine is getting up and working on the novel, first thing for a few hours. Lunchtime means food, email, whatever business needs to be addressed. Evenings are for other writing projects, and I've got plenty. My focus and drive vanished after I returned home, but they're coming back.

In an earlier interview about Dermaphoria, you said that you did around 20 drafts to get it down, now that you've got the first draft of your new book down, do you think it will take the same? How do you think your process has changed?

I wrote this book almost entirely longhand this time around, re-working each page as I wrote it. There isn't a set of linear footprints telling me exactly how many drafts I've done; some parts have been re-written more than others, in multiple iterations until I had a finished working draft. This forced me to slow down and think about each line more carefully. I'm letting the prose breathe a lot more this time around, rather than firing the reader out of a cannon (the way I opened my first two). I typically have two or three notepads laid out, or use distinct pages from a notebook. On the first, I rough out a line, over and over, shuffling my word choices until I have it right. Sometimes it works immediately, other times it takes me half a page. Once I have it, I transcribe it to a fresh page, go back to the first and tackle the next line. When the second page has a full, finished paragraph, I cut through that. Polishing every line one by one and then compiling them into a single paragraph creates what I call the Liberace effect. All of these perfect little sentences sparkle, and all that effort backfires. The paragraph sounds too much like writing because the prose overpowers the story. So I have to grind down the edges a bit, make those lines work together instead of clamor for the spotlight and derail the flow of the story.

I still work on my dialogue separately. Instead of extracting the dialogue from the chapter after I've written, or writing it after the narrative prose, I'm writing each chapter's dialogue first, this time around. This way I'm certain to have the characters—their words and actions—driving each chapter of the story, instead of having them pulled along by the narration. No phonetic spelling this time, except for "y'all" and "ain't." But no "wanna" or "gotta" or anything like that. This means choosing my characters' words more carefully, which means making their voices more distinct, the characters more nuanced. Same with similes and metaphors. I'm stripping those back to as few as I possibly can, which forces me to describe things more precisely in the first place, rather than leaning on a comparison to something else to back up whatever image I'm trying to convey.

There's other things I'm sure I'm forgetting, but the biggest change over the years has been working longhand. I like paper and ink, the tactile sensation of physically writing instead of a cursor on a screen. This makes me slow down and think more carefully about what I'm doing, and that's how I get happily lost in the process.

I don't put foil on my windows anymore, but I still stash or hide any clocks in my workspace. It's easier to fall down the creative rabbit hole if I'm not aware of time passing. I still outline rigorously, mapping out every beat of the story in as much detail as I can.

My process will likely never stop evolving. Complacency is hazardous to creative work.

You've given a lot of great recommendations over the years, do you have any books you've been reading recently that you love, or has the current book taken all focus?

"Kockroach," by Tyler Knox (William Lashner) wasn't exactly a recent read, but it's one of the few I can think of over the last few years I forced on everyone I could. Daniel Woodrell's "Winter's Bone" was brilliant, absolutely brilliant. Subdued but powerful writing, all in service of a very simple story. That's the kind of wordsmithing I aspire to do. I met Woodrell recently, and I was shaking like a schoolgirl. I just couldn't stop gushing. He took it in humble stride. Harry Crews, too. There's this fat anthology of his that's been staring at me from my bookshelf for ages. I finally cracked it open, and it's been my companion during my couch-surfing of late. Old Micky Spillane. And John Ridley. Now there's a solid noir writer, and truly underrated, in my opinion. Jennifer Egan's "The Keep" was easily the highlight of my reading in Bolivia.

Channing Tatum. On one side, I'm pumped that it's going to become a movie, on the other, I'm terrified. What are your thoughts? Are you going to have any input?

I'm optimistic about Channing Tatum. Plenty before him have overcome the low expectations set by their bone structure. Brad Pitt and Johnny Depp both come to mind. Both could have easily been typecast as pretty boys, but both have gained credibility and respect as actors over the years. Now that Tatum's firmly established himself as bankable, as someone who's not only a box office draw but who can open a movie, I think it's entirely possible he's looking to take the risks he was warned against early in his career. Yeah, I have high hopes for him. That's the good news.

The bad news is that my high hopes are in vain if the

Handbook film goes forward with the current script. No manner of casting could save this thing from certain disaster. The script is full of gunplay, fist fights and at least one car crash... loads of violence that has no basis in the story. It completely whitewashes Vincent's drug habit. Most of the original characters in the novel are gone; most of the characters in the script have no basis in the novel (especially the midget mob boss named Hugo). It's full of racist stereotypes and the treatment of Keara is appalling (she's a bipolar stripper whom the audience first meets when she's having a meltdown during her dancing shift... yeah, she's taking her clothes off and crying in front of a roomful of men). To say nothing of the unrealistic settings (such as the combination strip joint and casino in Vegas where Keara works), the atrocious, tinny dialogue and the misguided happy ending. Seriously, it's awful. The studio asked for my input, I gave it to them, and haven't heard anything but a brief email response since then.

IMDB says Dustin Hoffman attached, but it doesn't name the part and I haven't seen it confirmed elsewhere. I'm hoping now that Tatum is also producing the film, he'll have some say in the script and perhaps pull it away from the straight-to-streaming trash bin it's so destined for. As far as I'm concerned, Channing Tatum is the film's only hope.

If you were to get any piece of advice before you left your corporate job to write The Contortionist's Handbook, what would you tell yourself?

Get an agent.

Where do you see yourself as an author in the next 10, 20 years? Do you have any specific goals you want to hit?

I suck at the future. I rarely see beyond the next year. My eyes are usually right on the path at my feet. All that concerns me now is getting this rewrite finished, making up my mind about the title and getting it out to agents. Then writing another book.

How important is education in regards to your writing?

Education is critical, but that education doesn't always come from the classroom. I learn mostly by reading and writing, but also by observing and empathizing. Life happens in the blandest suburbia as much as the Parisian Left Bank.

How do you know when a book is "finished?"

I don't. I hit a stopping point of course, when I've written out everything in my outline and added a bunch of brainstorms along the way, then re-written it over and over. But with enough time, I can look back at something and find more work to be done. So I channel that into my next story.

What are your thoughts on basing characters on real people?

I assume you mean real people from my own life, and not famous public figures or people from history. I'm a novelist, not a journalist, so that's not something I do (at least as far as whole characters are concerned). Plenty of other novelists do it, but there are some obvious pitfalls. There are legal issues, of course, which is why every novel has the disclaimer in the opening pages, the garlic above the doorpost to ward off lawsuits from ex-spouses or former employers. Even without the legal concerns, you're treading through some hazardous emotional territory by basing a character on someone you know. Unless that portrayal is wholly and completely flattering (thus making for a thin, predictable character), you're bound to hit some nerves.

But I do take pieces of people, yes. I absolutely hate head-to-toe physical descriptions of people in novels (especially when that description is making a point of how handsome/beautiful the character is).There are obvious exceptions, but most of the time that's just the author playing with dolls.

For me, everything a reader needs to know about a character physically can be found in their voice, movement, eyes and hands. Okay, I'll cheat and use hair color, sometimes.

A lot of the dialect I write is based on my parents and extended relatives, their manner of speaking; I'll borrow particularly striking physical details that make for good descriptions, most all of the time the eyes and the hands, like I said. My father's hands look like they've been through the apocalypse, so I've modeled a character's hands after his. For me, a person's eyes, voice and hands tell me their whole story... add the way they move, the way they carry themselves, the way they look at you and speak to you, you can build an entire character around those things.

Thank you,
Goat

Bio

Craig Clevenger was born in Dallas, Texas. He is the author of two novels, "The Contortionist's Handbook" (MacAdam/Cage, 2002) and "Dermaphoria" (MacAdam/Cage, 2005). He currently lives in San Francisco. www.craigclevenger.com

Michael Kun

What comes to mind when you hear, "Mourning Goats?"

I think immediately of Mourning Goat and Takei, the wonderful 1960s Saturday morning cartoon series from Japan. As I recall, Takei Yunoshi was an orphan boy who ran away one evening and stumbled upon a sad billy goat (Mourning Goat) by a river. Mourning Goat was also an orphan, and, though a billy goat, he could speak several languages and knew Morse Code. The two became fast friends and traveled the countryside together, eating plants and uncooked fish and solving mysteries along the way. I believe the Harlem Globetrotters appeared in one episode. Of course, I may be mistaken about some of this. Perhaps all.

You were the first author at MacAdam Cage to have a three book deal, what did this mean to your career and what was it like working with the press?

The three-book deal with MacAdam Cage came on the heels of The Locklear Letters. The book was getting some attention, largely from BookSense and Amazon, and we were waiting for the book to take off and become an international bestseller so I could quit my job and travel the world, letting people kiss my hand and buy me drinks and cake, as I understand they are wont to do with renowned authors. We're still waiting. Especially for the cake.

I don't remember much about the negotiation other than that MacAdam Cage wanted to lock me up for three books (which sounded great to me since my next three books were nearly complete) and that their draft contract included a term whereby I would receive a huge bonus if one of the three books made it to #1 on the New York Times bestsellers list. I knew that wasn't going to happen, so we renegotiated the contract to provide that

I would receive the same enormous bonus if I became the heavy-weight boxing champion of the world, which seemed equally plausible. I am proud to say that, to my knowledge, I am the only author to negotiate such a clause with any publisher. And, as a lawyer, I can tell you that the clause is air tight. (Not incidentally, that clause gives me an excuse to eat whatever and whenever I want because I need to keep my weight up. After all, I don't get the bonus if I become the middleweight champion. Just heavy-weight. The contract is very explicit on that point).

I enjoyed my relationship with MacAdam Cage. I know they have fallen on some rough times, as have many publishers, and I hope they pull out of it. My favorite memory of my time with MacAdam Cage was the 2003 Book Expo in Los Angeles, where I live and work. David Poindexter, the publisher, arranged for a dinner for their authors who were attending the Expo. I was there to promote The Locklear Letters, my first book in 13 years, which most of the other authors were too young to have even heard of. Among the group at dinner were Audrey Niffeneggar (The Time Traveler's Wife), Craig Clevenger (The Contortionist's Handbook), Mark Dunn (Ella Minnow Pea), and Amanda Eyre Ward (Sleep Toward Heaven). It was a very impressive group, and I've read and enjoyed each of their books since (and recommend them all). The reason I mention it, though, is that there was a spirit of camaraderie among the group that you often don't see among writers. No competitiveness, no back-biting, but the opposite. It felt like a team. Audrey and I have lost touch over the years, though I have enjoyed watching her tremendous success, but Craig, Mark and Amanda became and have remained my friends.

You never officially studied writing in college, has it always been a passion of yours? What sparked the first words?

Actually, I did study writing in college, I just didn't major in it. I studied in the writing seminars program at the Johns Hopkins University under Stephen Dixon.

It's actually a funny story how that came about, though, and I apologize in advance if it sounds self-congratulatory. I hadn't intended to take any writing classes at Hopkins, but I wrote a column for the campus newspaper that started receiving a bit of attention. After reading them, Steve tracked me down at my part-time job to invite me to take some of his classes. (My part-time job was working in the kiosk in the student union that sold candy, cigarettes and newspapers. Although I'm not sure I should say "sold" since I don't recall ever actually charging anyone for anything). I expressed my concern to Steve about the structure of creative writing classes — I didn't like the idea of being told to write about my grandmother one week, then to write about my dog the next week — and Steve said, "Listen, you can ignore whatever assignment I give the class and write whatever you want. Just don't tell anyone." Or at least that's how I remember it. So I took classes with Steve for 3 years, wrote whatever I wanted, and got some very helpful feedback from him. His comments were often longer than the stories themselves. Eventually, Steve submitted one of my stories to Daniel Menaker at The New Yorker, and while that story was not accepted, that gave me the belief that someone, somewhere, might want to publish something I'd written.

In any event, not only did I study with Steve, but I'm proud to say I was his favorite student until Rosemary Mahoney came along, but I can't complain about that. She's a better writer than I, and has published a few exceptional books, including Whoredom in Kimmage.

By the way, if your readers aren't familiar with Stephen Dixon, I'd suggest they start with his short story collection, Thirteen Stories. As you may know, he came this close to winning the National Book Award for his novels Frog and Interstate some time ago, but I'm not sure I'd recommend those at first to readers who aren't familiar with Steve or his work.

And if Stephen Dixon should happen to stumble upon this

interview, I say, "Hey, Steve. Hope you're enjoying your retirement. Thanks again for your help. And for helping me pad my GPA. And for the nice jacket blurb for The Locklear Letters. In that order."

Working full-time and writing a novel is hard, how do you make it happen when your full-time job is being an attorney?

I know you don't want to hear this, but my job, my law firm (Epstein, Becker & Green), my clients and my cases come before my writing. I have people counting on me. I have a wife and a daughter, both of whom seem to like me, and we couldn't live for very long on what I make writing. And I have partners and clients who need me to devote my attention and creativity to the matters I'm handling because, in the practice of law, any slip-up or oversight can be costly, particularly in litigation. If I have spare time at night or on the weekends, and if I have the inspiration, I write. If I don't, I don't. Fortunately, to date, that's worked out fine.

What is your favorite style to write in? Novels, short stories or non-fiction, and why?

Non-fiction is the easiest for me, particularly the type of non-fiction that I write, which is usually about sports. Writing about pro football for www.washingtonpost.com/theleague is a pleasure because it comes very naturally.

But "easiest" isn't necessarily "favorite," is it? My favorite would be short stories because of the challenge to do something, to affect a reader, in a relatively short space. Not incidentally, there's more room for experimentation and less of a sense of failure if the experiment blows up in your face. If you read my short story collection, Corrections to My Memoirs, you can hear a few of those explosions.

I love the piece you wrote on Why Lawyers Write Novels, do you think anything like that could ever happen in the field?

Thanks, Goat, I'm glad you enjoyed the piece. The idea that the legal profession needs an overhaul isn't a new or profound one, but I'm sad to say it's unlikely to happen in my lifetime. Simply put, the profession has no incentive to police itself more closely that it already does. Incompetent, dishonest or unethical lawyers only create more work and more profit for the other lawyers. If the good lawyers drove out the bad ones, the good ones would have less work to do, which of course translates to less money. To the extent the legal system is set up to benefit lawyers, it's working perfectly.

You proposed to your wife with the dedication page from You Poor Monster, that's pretty epic, is she your first reader? If not, who is?

I did propose to Amy with the dedication page of You Poor Monster. I gave her a draft of the novel on her birthday and asked her to turn to that page, where it read, "To my wife." She's pretty funny, and I only learned later that she nearly responded, "I didn't know you were married." Now that I think of it, I'm not sure she actually said, "Yes."

My wife is one of my first readers these days, but not the only one. It's not that I don't trust her opinion, but we all know she's so damned lucky to be married to me that she'd never tell me if something stunk. (Please imagine I just winked as I said that). She's one of the people I asked to take a look at my new book, Everybody Says Hello. The others are my old friends Bert Johnson and Gary Campbell.

Like many writers, I've been very fortunate to have had a number of people who were willing to read my work over the years, and to give me feedback, and I always worry that I've never thanked them enough.

In college, it was Kathryn Rhett, who's gone on to have a career as a poet, memoirist and editor. I believe she's teaching creative writing in Pennsylvania these days. (If she should stumble upon this, I say, "Thanks, Kath").

When I was in law school and for several years afterward, I relied upon my friend and law school classmate Susan Stevens, without whom I can honestly say that I never would have had a word published. I know if she ever reads this she will accuse me of being dramatic, but it's true. I could pass a polygraph on that. ("Thanks, Sue").

After that, I relied upon my good friends Andy Bienstock and Gary Campbell to read and comment on my writing. ("Thanks, guys").

There were also a couple of ex-girlfriends who gave me their thoughts, too, but if you break up with me, you don't get your name mentioned in "Mourning Goats." Sorry, but those are the rules.

Do you have time to read for pleasure? What are some recommendations for the readers?

I do have some time to read for pleasure, mostly late at night or when I'm traveling. Unfortunately, I've been suffering from "reader's block" for a while. I buy books with the full intention of reading them, then put them aside if I can't get into them after 10 or 12 pages. It's not the books or the authors. It's me.

That said, there are two books I've read recently that I recommend.

First is Maile Meloy's short story collection Both Ways Is The Only Way I Want It. She's a remarkable writer. Her writing seems so effortless, and she has the rare ability to make you care about a character within a few sentences.

The second is Stephen Elliott's The Adderall Diaries. The book isn't up my alley in any way. I normally steer clear of memoirs, and memoirs about drug use and violence wouldn't usually intrigue me. But Stephen and I used to share an editor, and we've met a few times over the years, so I picked it up just to support another writer. Within a page I was hooked. It's a unique, compelling book, and Stephen's lack of faith in his own memories and willingness to share adventures that most of us would hide forever is admirable.

I also love Mo Willems' Leonardo the Terrible Monster. It's a kids' book that I've read to my daughter Paige far too many times, but never tire of.

Have any/all of your books been optioned for movies? Which would you like to see done most? Least?

The Locklear Letters has been optioned for a movie several times. I honestly don't know who has the option these days. There was a brief period of time when Pat O'Brien, Heather Locklear and I were talking about producing the movie together, but that never panned out. I'd still love to see The Locklear Letters turned into a movie, but the one I'd really like to see made into a movie is You Poor Monster. Granted, Charlie Kauffman might need to write the script to keep the two competing narratives going, but I can picture it in my mind. For some reason I always seen Tom Hanks as Shoogey.

I have no interest in seeing The Baseball Uncyclopedia: The Movie. Nor should anyone else.

On your website it says you're currently working on a new book (my favorite title in the list is Everybody Says Hello), what can you tell us about it?

I just finished the final draft of Everybody Says Hello a couple weeks ago. It's a stand-alone Sid Straw epistolary novel. Sid was the main character in The Locklear Letters. In Everybody Says Hello, he relocates to California for a new job after his girlfriend leaves him. I'd like to think that it's every bit as entertaining as The Locklear Letters, but perhaps a bit more poignant. And, candidly, I hope the book finds a nice audience because I'd like to revisit the character every 5 years or so. I could see Sid Straw becoming my Rabbit Angstrom.

You have your website, facebook, and email address very accessible to your fans, have you had a lot of interaction since your second book? What do you see has changed since A Thousand Benjamins?

The way authors interact with their readers has changed completely since A Thousand Benjamins came out 20 years ago.

Then, if readers wanted to share some thoughts with an author, they'd have to mail a letter to the publisher and hope it got forwarded. Now, they can reach many writers instantaneously through websites or email. I don't know about other writers, but it makes my day to get a kind email from a reader. And I'm more than happy to call in to talk with a book club.

We recently interviewed Pat Walsh here at Mourning Goats, and was wondering if he's still your editor at MacAdam Cage and what your thoughts are about him.

Pat hasn't been my editor for a few years. As you may know, he left MacAdam Cage for a while, and I had different editors there for my last two books. Pat's a good guy and was always very supportive of my writing. I just saw him and David Poindexter, the publisher, when I was in San Francisco a few weeks back, and we all had a nice time catching up. Although, now that I think of it, my wallet was missing afterward.

Can you tell us a little bit about your uncyclopedias? Did you come up with the idea?

I had wanted to write a baseball book for some time, but none of my ideas were even getting a nibble from publishers. The quirky-obscure-writer-writes-quirky-stuff-about- baseball pitch was going nowhere. Then one night I had the idea of writing a book that would ostensibly debunk some commonly held notions about the game and calling it an "uncyclopedia." Seemed like a fun word that I thought I was making up. And The Baseball Uncyclopedia was born. Then The Football Uncyclopedia. I'm working on The Movie Uncyclopedia with my friends Lou Harry (The High-Impact Infidelity Diet), Theresa Hoiles (Love, Luck and Lore) and Eric Feinstein. Then I'm giving up on this uncyclopedia stuff.

I read a review on Amazon from a "past girlfriend" that said "Mike wrote two great books — A Thousand Benjamins and Our Poor Sweet Napoleon — then stopped writing. He won't talk about it, but he had his heart broken by a girl he went to

law school with and just lost the desire to write." Is there any truth to this? Also, is there anywhere to read Our Poor Sweet Napoleon?

Some of it is true, some of it isn't. And some of it she's just confused about. (And, yes, I can figure out who wrote that review. Terrific woman. Saw her at a book signing in Baltimore a few years back. Glad she's doing well).

Did I write two great books, A Thousand Benjamins and Our Poor Sweet Napoleon? Yes and no. I wrote them, but they're not great books. I still appreciate all of the kind and generous reviews for A Thousand Benjamins, and I'm truly sorry if I haven't lived up to the predictions of those reviewers, but today it seems very clearly a book written by a young man trying to sound wiser than he really was. As for Our Poor Sweet Napoleon, it was serialized over 36 weeks in The City Paper in Baltimore back in the early 1990s. I reworked it over the course of 10 years or so, and it eventually became You Poor Monster. I'm sure someone somewhere still has the original, serialized version, though God knows why anyone would want to read it now. I certainly don't. It was unwieldy and vain. It was written by a young writer who had let his reviews go to his head.

Did I stop writing for a while after those books? Yes.

Was it because I had my heart broken by a girl I went to law school with and lost the desire to write? No. I did have my heart broken around that time, but not by anyone I went to law school with, and I didn't lose the desire to write. I kept revising Our Poor Sweet Napoleon, but just didn't have much time to write because of my work.

You co-authored two books, what was the process like in both of them? How hard was it to agree on topics and/or ideas to put in the book?

You're referring to The Baseball Uncyclopedia and The Football Uncyclopedia. They were both a pleasure to work on, and I rarely butted heads with my co-authors on either. In both cases, we would email each other various sections, then share feedback, until we had a final working draft. From there, we sat down together and did a final edit.

You have some very loyal fans, if you read the reviews on Amazon.com, they actually bash the people that have given bad reviews of your books, have you perused the reviews? What are your thoughts?

Over the years I suspect I have seen most, if not all, of those Amazon reviews. Friends email the links to me all the time. There are some very kind ones, which I appreciate. And there are some that are not so kind. There's one reader who posts a venomous, one-star review of each of my books. I honestly don't know why he or she would keep reading anything of mine if he or she dislikes my writing so much. If I don't like a book, I'm not likely to pick up that writer's next book, let alone his next five. I suspect that he or she hasn't read any of them, but that it's someone I've crossed paths with personally or professionally who's using the anonymity of Amazon.com to get even with me. To the extent other readers have been watching my back, I'm touched. And if they want to step up and identify themselves, I'll buy them a drink.

I got a lot of your books on my kindle (already had them in hardcover, but the prices were so good I couldn't pass them up, just read The Locklear Letters, again!). What do you think about the way publishing is going?

It's a very strange time for publishing, isn't it, and it's hard to tell how much of what's happening is a result of the recession, declining interest or technology.

In many ways it's both the best of times and the worst of times to be a writer. If you're looking to get published in the traditional sense — hardcover books sold in brick-and-mortar stores — it's the worst of times. It's harder than ever to get a contract, let alone an advance you could live on. But if you just want to write something and share it with the world, it couldn't be easier or cheaper to do it. All you need is computer and a website.

As for e-books and e-readers and the impact they will have, I know no more than anyone else, and my feelings are very mixed. As a reader myself, I haven't purchased an e-reader yet, although I have to admit that I'm more intrigued than ever by iPads, Nooks and Kindles and may eventually give in and buy one, mostly for travel. The reason I haven't done so to date is that I enjoy bookstores too much. The experience of being in a bookstore is often more enjoyable to me than actually reading a book, and I would miss that. Similarly, I would miss the feel of holding a book in my hands. That said, as a writer, I know that e-books will be an important part of my future.

How e-books and e-readers will affect bookstores is another issue. Independent bookstores have been very kind to me over the years, and I've spent more than my fair share of time and money in them. (Two of my favorites off the top of my head — BookWorks in Albuquerque, New Mexico and Read Between The Lynes in Woodstock, Illinois). I want to see them continue to flourish, but e-books are a serious threat to them.

I know it's fashionable to trash the big chain bookstores, but I love Barnes & Noble and Borders, too. Not just because they have been very kind to me both nationally and locally, but because I enjoy the experience offered by their stores. No, not the coffee, but the selection and the roominess.

There's room for both the independents and the chains. And for Amazon, too. I know it's fashionable to trash Amazon for its impact on publishing, but I won't do that either. If the idea behind being a writer is to get your words in as many hands as possible, in many ways Amazon is the best thing to happen to writers in decades.

But e-books and e-readers change all of this. If they increase readers and sales, great. If they lead to the end of physical books and brick-and-mortar stores, terrible. If I had to predict the future, I don't see bookstores vanishing. There are too many of us who enjoy the experience of bookstores and of holding a book. But as e-readers inevitably become more popular, I suspect that the business models will change, and bookstores will have a different relationship with e-books.

I loved the letters on your website to co-workers, any plans for more? Have any of your co-workers ever realized that they were about them?

I was just fooling around, and I enlisted some help in faxing the fake letters to my co-workers remotely so they hopefully wouldn't figure out that they came from me. I don't know if I should be proud or offended that they figured it out immediately. I'm afraid I'm done with the fake letters to co-workers, at least for now. I'm trying to act more like an adult these days.

What is the best advice you can give to writers out there?

Write something. Anything. But just write. I can't tell you how many people I've met over the years who have introduced themselves as writers but who haven't written anything. I don't mean that they haven't published anything, but that they haven't written anything. They'll talk your ear off about an idea they have, and two years later they're still talking about the same idea, not having written a word. Don't be that person. Write. If you like it, keep it. If you don't like it, still keep it. You never know if your opinion of it will change.

What's next for Michael Kun? Do you see yourself retiring from law anytime soon to write full-time?

I hope that Everybody Says Hello will be out sometime in 2011 or early 2012 (April 16, 2012). The same for The Movie Uncyclopedia (TBA).

I've started work on a new novel called This Means War, but I'm not very far along and will likely have to change the title as I've seen there's a movie coming out soon with that title. I'm leaning toward calling it Ten (More) Commandments. I will probably talk myself out of that by the time you post this interview.

I hope to keep writing about the National Football League for www.thewashingtonpost.com/theleague, if they still want me and if Brett Favre doesn't have me bumped off. I haven't had too many kind things to say about him.

As for retirement, that's not going to happen for a long, long time. Our daughter is 4 years old. If I'm doing my math right, we've got 17 more years of food, clothing and tuition for that kid. But that's fine. She's a great kid, even if she has some odd plans for the future. She's already decided she want to be a writer when she grows up. A writer and an "ice ballerina," whatever that is.

How do you know when the book is finished?

I know this has infuriated some of the editors I've worked with over the years, but I don't consider a book to be finished until it's been sent off the printer. It's still a work-in-progress until then, at least in my mind. There have been a few occasions where I've even tweaked a book after the advance review copies were printed, but before the final printing. Some of those last-minute tweaks have been minor, but some have been more significant. There was a fairly important sentence that I added to You Poor Monster just before it was sent off to the printer, although now I don't recall precisely which one it was. The same thing withThe Locklear Letters. But once the book is printed in final, where the only way you could make a change would be to burn all of the copies and then reprint the whole thing, well, then it's safe to say it's done. Then I can put it behind me and move on. Which isn't to say that months or even years later I don't think of something I wish I could change.

What are three mistakes you made as a beginning writer?

Great question. I'd have to say my three biggest mistakes were:

Allowing myself to be influenced too much by the writers I admired. If you'd like to see some really terrible Salinger or Vonnegut knockoffs, I believe I can dig them out of storage for you. Some of my early stories were just lousy with those writers' unique mannerisms. But so it goes.

Making rules for myself. When I first started to take writing seriously, I had a list of rules I swore I would live by. Most of them have gone flying out the window over the past 25+ years. First, I swore I would never write about writers because that was too self-aggrandizing and because their lives tend to be too insulated; I have since written at least three books about writers or aspiring writers. Second, I swore I would never write about lawyers because I hated the way other lawyer/writers try to make the profession appear more interesting than it really is; lawyers have since appeared in at least four of my books, though I'd like to think they play a strikingly different role than they do in other novels. Third, I swore I would never write in the first person; no idea why I came up with that rule or what it was intended to accomplish. Fourth, I swore I would never write about drug use; that was a reaction to some of my contemporaries (who shall remain nameless), who seemed to rely upon drug use when they reach a roadblock in the plot or to somehow substitute for character development. Fifth, I swore I would never use foul language in one of my books, despite the fact that I personally curse more than anyone outside of a David Mamet, play; that, too, was meant to try to set myself apart from some of my contemporaries and make sure that I didn't use shortcuts.

Taking criticism too personally. I don't write traditional, linear fiction. I don't know why I thought I could please everyone.

Do you have a favorite part of being a writer?

There's nothing like the day a shipment of author's copies of a new book shows up on the front porch. Writers who claim they don't get a thrill out of seeing their names on the front covers of a stack of new books are liars, plain and simple.

Thank you,
Goat

Bio

Michael Kun is the acclaimed author of five novels, including You Poor Monster (a Barnes and Noble "Discover Great New Writers" selection and a Borders "Original Voices" selection), The Locklear Letters (a BookSense #1 selection), and Everybody Says Hello. He is also the author of the short story collection Corrections to My Memoirs and the co-author of several non-fiction sports books, and he is a contributor to The Washington Post's online National Football League coverage. Michael is a long-time attorney who practices labor and employment law. He lives in Los Angeles with his wife Amy and their daughter Paige.

5 Questions about Author Promotion with Caleb J. Ross

What's important about self-promotion in today's market?

These days, all promotion is self-promotion. Reality TV and social networks have trained creators and consumers to expect direct access to the minds behind the goods. Couple this mind-set with the ever-diminishing advertising budgets allotted to authors and musicians, and it becomes obvious that self-promotion is simply part of the media consumption model, not a different paradigm altogether, as some have suspected. I don't mean to imply that every writer has to be a whore—even if only talking to a stranger about your work, that's still self-promotion—but to effectively create a sense of need or excitement the human story, the "self" part of promotion, is important.

Do you think that e-books make selling books, easier or harder?

E-books make the process of selling much easier, but the idea of e-books hasn't yet taken over. So, in terms of distribution and overhead, e-books are amazing. I can have business cards printed up with a QR code that links directly to purchase sites for my books quite easily, much easier than keeping a warehouse full of print books. However, the market isn't 100% sold on e-books yet meaning most readers still demand print books.

E-books definitely make it easier to try different promotional tactics, for sure. For example, I recently did a print book giveaway at Goodreads.com. I offered to the 400+ entrants (over a 7 day period) free e-book copies of some of my other books if they filled out a quick questionnaire. I could not have done that if e-books didn't exist. What came of it is confirmation of something I've long suspected: Goodreads.com is a great place to find readers.

E-books have also allowed me to easily distribute collected

stories and individual stories on my own without having to rely on the blessing of a publisher. Publishers still make sense for much of the publishing market place, but sometimes I want to do things on my own just to see how it works. Publishers, the big ones anyway, aren't willing to experiment.

How can a writer sell him- or herself?

To sell anything a person has to be one of two personalities (or a mixture of both): 1) a competitive weasel who only cares about the hunt, or 2) a person who is genuinely interested in the product and honestly couldn't care less if the product ever actually sold. That #2 personality, that's all about passion. A writer should be passionate about his books. If one speaks passionately about something, others will follow. Also, a writer needs to be genuinely interested in the literary community at large. Participation in blog comments, forums, social networks, etc. goes a long way to put a face behind the product. Readers can smell bullshit. A writer must be authentically passionate about writing. I'm lucky enough to genuinely enjoy reading communities, so I feel comfortable talking about writing (not just my own writing) and reading (not just my own books) to strangers online. Writers need to be passionate.

Is social media the new marketing department?

Social media is definitely an important component of marketing but isn't a total replacement. Social media is about putting a face behind a product, but there still should be measures out there to put a product behind a product, so to speak.

In a Venn diagram of marketing, social media would be the intersection of book, author, and traditional marketing, with weight being given to the author and book portions. Traditional marketing never really capitalized on the author as a personality (until the author died, of course, so that a legacy could be culti-vated according to the publisher's wishes). Social media allows for that missing component.

Books, especially, have much to gain from social media. It has been a long-held belief in publishing that newspaper reviews, author tours, in-store promotions, these things sell relatively few books. What really sells books is word-of-mouth. A friend telling a friend telling a friend. Social media is basically a giant word-of-mouth platform.

What are you working on that you're excited about?

I've been working on a collection of four novellas with some author friends, which may see light sometime in 2012. I'm damn excited about that. My portion is more genre crime than I've written before, but I had a lot of fun with it so there may be more from me in the future.

I've been focusing a lot on promotion over the last year so I am really excited to dive back into writing. I've written a few short stories during the previous year, but nothing truly long-form. I'd like to get back to one of the many aborted novels I have gathering virtual dust on my computer.

Thank you,
Goat

Bio

Caleb J Ross has been published widely, both online and in print. He is the author of Charactered Pieces: Stories (OW Press), Stranger Will: A Novel (Otherworld_Publications, 2011), I Didn't Mean to Be Kevin: A Novel (Black Coffee Press, 2012), and As a Machine and Parts (Aqueous_books, 2011).Visit his official page at www.calebjross.com, his Twitter feed at @calebjross, his Facebook at facebook.com/rosscaleb and his Google+ at http://bit.ly/CalebGoogle.

Rob Roberge

What comes to mind when you hear, "Mourning Goats?"

Well, when I first heard of this (very cool, by the way) series, it made me think of the band The Mountain Goats, maybe because it sounded sort of the same, and I like some of their stuff a lot, and a friend of mine plays with them sometimes.

Then, after reading the interviews, what came to my mind was this page. It had replaced The Mountain Goats, once I knew what it was.

But, it also makes me think of Alonzo Mourning, retired from the NBA and starting a goat-breeding business called "Mourning Goats." Cause, you know, that would probably be the name of Alonzo Mourning's Goat-Breeding business, wouldn't you think? Or "Mourning's Goats"...he might like the sound of the possessive. I can't speak for him. We had a falling out years ago. I can't say much (it's part of the settlement). But, let's just say it involved us both being involved with a very famous and beautiful Hip-Hop star (again, I'd like to name her...but, the settlement) and it didn't end well. It got ugly. This happens surprisingly often when unknown writers and rich NBA stars compete for the affections of beautiful, ridiculously famous women. Much more often than you'd guess. Just last year, my friend Tod Goldberg and LeBron James had quite the dust-up at AWP. I shouldn't talk about that, though. It's not really my place. All I can really say is don't mess with Tod Goldberg, or you might end up so rattled that, even months later, you'll play surprisingly poorly in the NBA Finals.

Though Tod is hardly as unknown as me...he's a big-time famous writer. But still. My point was...well, you don't want NBA stars and fiction writers in the same room unless you're the kind of person who likes adult-sized trouble.

But, you know, back to Alonzo for a moment. He might call

his Goat-Breeding business "Zo's Goats," but that doesn't sound as cool. Maybe if he starts a Goat-Breeding business and uses your name, you can sue his rich ass and make some serious cheddar. But the settlement will include a gag-order, I can assure you.

You have fantastic reviews of your books on Amazon.com, how hard is it to not think about them when you write?

Those are probably all me under a variety of fifty fake names.

Seriously? It's easy not to think about them when I write. F. Scott Fitzgerald said (and he may have been quoting someone, so it may not originate with him, but he was the first I heard say/write it) that if you believe the good ones, you have to believe the bad ones.

I'm very flattered by them. And I do think of them when I think I suck. Though, on days I think I suck, they're of no comfort because any praise I get on the dark days, I tend to think is wrong.

But, I really don't think I've ever thought of them while writing, or even when I'm working on a project, but not sitting that moment writing. I wrote for a lot of years before anyone read anything of mine, save for the editors rejecting those pieces. So, my training had little, if anything, to do with worrying about an audience I didn't have.

When I write, I think about the writing.

Actually, that's not quite true. When I revise and edit, I think about the writing, narrative theory, issues of craft, and so on. When I write, I try to clear my head, listen to the language, and try to think of something that would happen next that would excite me, if I were reading the book. Writing is very "in the moment" for me. It's some of the only time I'm not worrying about the future or regretting the past. Writing is a lot like sex. Somehow it's become a sort of Zen-state for me, where I can be totally in the moment. And thinking doesn't have much to do with it at that point.

How did you get involved in restoring old medical devices?

In all honesty (and why not just be honest?), some friends of ours had this really electric cool sex toy they showed us called a Violet Wand.

(And just for the record, if anyone who's in charge of the ethics clause in my wife's contract is reading this, I'm talking about another wife. I've had eleven. Maybe sixteen, over the years. I've lost track. I'm the Liz Taylor of incredibly obscure writers...this parenthetical is less honest than the rest of this answer, but you can't be too careful these days).

But, back to your Q: A Violet Wand is kind of a variation of a Tesla coil (not exactly, but this isn't a science class, and I'm not bright enough to teach such a class, anyway), and it can give off a really mild, warm sensation, or it can be turned up (safely) to zap the hell out of a person. Or anywhere in between those two sensations. And they're really beautiful...they use (mostly) Argon gas in a vacuum blown glass attachment, and they glow a stunning kind of purple/violet (hence the name) when they're turned on, and the gas is excited. The glass attachment plugs into the hand-held device that is black (plastic now—Bakelite back in the day) about the size of a D-Battery flashlight. They had a bunch of different shapes of glass...one that looks like a comb that was supposed to cure baldness. This wacky shaped one that was for your heart. This was VERY quack science, as far as working medically. Other gasses in the glass give off different colors. Neon is a kind of orange.

Not often, but every once in a while, some of the glass parts were Mercury-coated in the old ones. They're not clear, but the color of the Mercury in an old thermometer. Obviously, you shouldn't be running electrically charged, heated Mercury over your skin. Those are the attachments you don't use, and actually should get rid of safely. Mercury poisoning can make a person as whacked and loony and bat-shit crazy as Michele Bachmann. Or her husband. He's even loonier, maybe, but that's a tough race to call.

Anyway, new Violet Wands were really expensive and we were kind of broke, so I did some research and found out the new ones were just a modern version of this electric health/medical device from the 1920's-1930's called a Violet Ray. At the time, they were dirt cheap on eBay, so I bought a few, figured out how they worked and restored the best of the three, and re-wired it with a ground plug for safety.

And then, I ended up finding out about some other cool stuff—like Electro Muscle Stimulant Units (sort of a higher powered and more Dr. Frankenstein-y version of a TENS unit they use today for muscle rehab in physical therapy). There are unsafe ways to use those, so anyone out there reading this who is going to run out and buy them, read up on how to use them safely.

After that, I found a few others that were just kind of cool-looking. It's odd...people were CRAZY for electric medical devices in the 1920's and into the 30's...electricity in homes was a little new, as more towns and cities installed AC current, and people seemed to think (or were told by ads and media of the day) that electricity could do everything and anything. So, a bunch of them are just cool looking and have no practical application unless someone wanted to lobotomize themselves, or read their personality by the bumps on their head with a Phrenology cap (very cool, if very stupid). I had a Phrenology cap and sold it. It's one of my great regrets. One should never sell a Phrenology cap...they don't grow on trees. They're not something you trip over at Costco.

But, originally? I got into them for sex. It's why I do a lot of things.

Do you think there's a connection between writing fiction and writing lyrics?

When I write prose, I put a lot of pressure on myself and set the bar pretty high.

With music, the bar's a little lower...I'm having fun with my friends and making noise and playing to bigger crowds than writers tend to get...getting to tour...I wish writers would tour like bands. It's a hell of a lot more fun. Actually, Craig Clevenger and I are thinking of doing some version of a group tour, a travelling literary freak show. Wordapalosa or something.

Back to lyrics: Sometimes I come up with a really good line here or there, but often, they're (the lyrics) the thing that carries the melody and keeps the song from being an instrumental.

It's hard to say, though. Good question. I do know for certain that I'm far more nervous/uncomfortable playing my songs solo with an acoustic guitar than I am doing a reading. So, maybe it's just that I have more confidence and faith in my prose.

In your interview on The Rumpus, you say that you write to understand who you are, can you expand on that? I completely agree.

Yeah...I'm not sure exactly how to explain it. Maybe an example would do the job: From 1996-2003, I wrote two novels, maybe ten to fifteen stories that I kept (and probably double that in failed ones) a few screenplays, and maybe five plays. It was probably the most sustained productive stretch (by word count, at least) of my life.

And only sometime in 2004, did I realize that, while each writing project was a different narrative with different plots and characters, there was one enormous thread they all shared. In a way, everything I wrote in those seven years was about me trying to deal with the horror of life changing in an instant. And thatfear—of loss of everything than matters being gone in a second—ran though all those narratives—some overtly, some not.

They were all ABOUT something else, but they shared this fear in some way. And I didn't realize it until after I'd written them all. And that fear was triggered by two events in my life where everything, as I understood it, DID fall apart in an instant (once, a very long time ago) and where it seemed about to happened (maybe six months before this stretch of writing) when there was the enormous threat of a life-altering event. An emergency surgery on the person I love the most in the world. Luckily, that one didn't end badly, but the threat was there. And that can trigger PTSD, if you have it, where the initial fracture (of life/security/meaning) comes back at you, like it's all happening again, not in memory, but all in the same moment. It's a freakish brain anxiety overload. So, all those things I wrote were VERY different from each other in plot, character, structure and language. But the one thing they all shared was this enormous fear of loss that I was working my way (unconsciously) through with the writing. I didn't have any idea I was doing that, and I like it that way.

But, I think (or I fear) that stuff's only interesting for the writer (so I apologize for going on about it a bit), and maybe his or her friends. Telling people what you discovered from your own writing is a little like people telling you their dreams. No one cares. Nor should they. It's whether the narrative (in whatever form or genre) works or not.

But, in general, it's a pretty amazing part of the process for me. I write the best narrative I can...I try to write the book that I would most like to read. I don't ever think about theme—the word alone makes me cringe. And I don't, to paraphrase Gordon Lish's wonderful observation, ever want my narratives be "reduced to meaning." Stories and novels are bigger than meaning. They're like living things.

I never think about what a story "means." I find that a reductive and boring way to look at the gig. I prefer to look at how they exist, what differentiates how they exist from other stories. But, you know, it works for a lot of people...theme and meaning and so on. I'm not interested in being prescriptive. Whatever works for anyone else? Cool. It's just not a way of looking at narrative that's very interesting to me.

Not only do you have an MFA, but you teach in an MFA program, what do you think about teaching the craft?

I love it—though I'm doing a little too much of it at the moment. If I won the lottery or something, I'd still teach. Of course I'd have to play the lottery. But I'd do it less. However, it's a great job. I learn a lot from my students. And, hopefully, I pass something along from my experience in the craft (and the business) that helps them tell their stories better than they did before we got to work together.

Also, it keeps you sharp (or, I should say it keeps me sharp), as I'm always breaking stories down, trying to see and share how they work (or where and how they don't). And when you teach, you give a lot of advice. And then, sometimes, I realize I'm giving good advice and not following it myself. It keeps me relentlessly challenging my aesthetic. It's very healthy to try and explain how a narrative works, and then try to show how it can be applied to everyone's work in a different way (because they're unique, so their stories should be, as well). And I'm always learning, if I pay attention to what I'm asking my students to pay attention to.

You said in an interview on The Hipster Book Club that you write very autobiographical, do you think it's possible to not include yourself in your stories?

Yes and no. Part of a long book I'm working on is set in the Bikini Islands in 1946, when the United States moved (temporarily, we told/lied to them) the people who'd lived there for hundreds of years off their home island so that we could test atom bombs. We bombed the shit out of this little atoll for seven or eight years with atom bombs. Then, in 1954, we tested nuclear bombs there, and the island has been poisoned, is still too hot with Cesium 137 for anyone to live there, and the native people live on a shitty, much smaller island that we left them on.

Anyway, in that book, I have the POV of a woman, who clearly wouldn't be me. And of a soldier in 1946 (again, I have no experience like that), and then 4 more POV's all the way up to 2006. If I write from the POV of a woman or a 20 year old soldier exposed to radiation in 1946, it isn't autobiographical in the strict sense that the thing happened to me in my life. But they all are autobiographical in a way they're all processed through my world view, the people I find interesting enough to write a novel about, the plots that resonate with me and my history with and use of language. Stuff like that.

How did you get in to teaching? When you went for your MFA, was that the plan all along?

I'll answer the second one first. Nope—teaching was not the plan. I went to the MFA program to learn how to be a better writer. Going for any other reason isn't wise, I think.

Teaching? Well, I'd hated every real/honest job I'd ever had. So, I thought I'd try it. I got into teaching Composition at a crappy, creepy religious school (I have no idea what religion it was...they all kind of blend to me...religions are like watching Australian Rules Football on, like, ESPN III to me. I can watch it forever and still have no idea of how it works, how they keep score and what anything means at the end of it) where the head of the English department was this dusty 60 year old woman who threatened to fire me for wearing red Chuck Taylors. I had to wear a tie. A tie!? Ties are for using in a pinch if you don't have any fun bondage gear. So, it didn't start out so well.

But then we moved to Long Beach in 1995, and I had a terrible editing job. I was line-editing 1,200 pages 60 hours a week for 17 grand a year. I was good at it, but it was killing me. My friend Rachel Resnick recommended me (for which I'm enormously grateful) to Linda Venus at the UCLA Extension Writers' Program in 1996. Linda took a chance on me (I only had maybe 3-4 published stories..so, I'm enormously grateful to Linda as well), and it was a fabulous program, and it turned out I was good at the job. It was probably the first job of my life that I didn't despise. Except for playing guitar, but that wasn't really a job. I'm just not made for real jobs. I stunk at every job I had before this one. Absolutely dreadful employee.

And I had some awful jobs, too, but they could have been worse. Like, in some ancient kingdoms, they had a food-taster, who would take a bite of the meal. If he dropped dead, the King's dinner had been poisoned, so the king wouldn't eat it. If he lived…well, he still had to do that job the next meal. That's a bad job.

What do you think about where publication is going, with e-readers, etc.?

Honestly, I have no idea. I love physical books—they are special, nearly sacred to me, as objects, let alone what's on their pages. Books saved me, in many ways. Can a text on a Kindle or an iPad save someone's life? Probably. It doesn't have to be the object it's been. But I will miss it. I'll be the last guy on my block with my Horseless Carriage, while my neighbors zip around in their Model T's.

I write books. I promote them (which I love)…traveling/getting to do shows/readings. I'll bust my ass for a publisher who had the faith to partner up with me and my work. But, how they are going to get to the reader/what delivery method? Really no idea. I probably should pay attention to that stuff, but I'm not good at business and money stuff. I'm kind of a stooge, in many ways. Career-wise/trends in publishing and that kind of thing, for sure. Stooge.

Do you think that writing has helped you move forward as a person? It sounds like your late teens forward was pretty rough.

Well, everyone has their troubles. My problem was how I choose to deal with my troubles. I self-medicated quite a bit and lost a lot of years. It's a typical course—at first drugs worked and made me feel good for the first time in my life. And then they stopped working. It would have been nice if I could have stopped doing them when they stopped working, but I decided to give them many more years of trying. I just could not manage life when I wasn't loaded. But, eventually, you can get to a place where you're not the talented, young, promising fuck-up who's the life of the party...you're the person who's hurt everyone around you and has hurt yourself, for years. Eventually, if you're lucky, you realize, deeply, that you don't know anything. You're being selfish with other people's lives, and you have to change and learn how to live, or you'll probably die or go to jail.

I also believed in that drunk/addict/suffering artist horseshit, and thought it justified my behavior. I'd be kicked out of bands, lost friends...I was kind of a train wreck. I'd been with some wonderful women and let them down in a variety of ways and they would get upset, they would suffer, and I'd kind of float around saying, "hey you knew I was a royal fuck-up when we met. Public record." It turns out that's not so charming in the long run. Go figure.

But writing? Once I was able to do it again (I hadn't written for years, at one point) I think writing helped me lead a more engaged life. It makes me pay attention. Listen. Be in the moment. Empathize—narrative prose (fiction/memoir) is an art of empathy enacted in language, for me. And that's powerful and essential. Most hideous human behavior is at least partially a result of a thorough lack of empathy for others. To learn and respect without judgment what it is to be in someone else's skin and head. It's good for me. I think it's good for a culture, too, and if we lose too many more readers and continue dumbing down our instant gratification/reality-TV/celebrity-obsessed culture, I truly think we're fucked.

What was it like winning the 2003 Instructor of the Year Award in creative writing?

Just getting to teach has been one of the many unexpected blessings of my life. I had no idea how good it could feel to have a positive impact on someone's life (I'd been much more proficient at being a negative influence). So, being noticed for being a good teacher? It made me feel appreciated. So much of the writing life is rejection, not much money and a lot of time alone. So, it was really nice. I work hard. I care a lot about teaching and I give a lot, because my best teachers gave me a lot. You owe to people the best you've received from other people, if that makes sense.

Saul Bellow said, "A writer is a reader moved to emulation." And I think a teacher is a student moved to emulation, as well. It's a different art form than writing and I think a lot of writers don't see as a different discipline—the writing and the teaching of writing.

How do you find time for it all? You write, sing in 3 bands, restore old amps, teach, and are married; I'm tired just writing that out.

You know, until about 5 years ago, I did all those things, and could somehow manage to do them all at the same time. Not now. I need to change my bio-ha! Maybe it's age. Maybe it's just that I have the biggest teaching load I've ever had this term. So, that's only allowed for squirreling away time for writing and my relationships, and the rest of the stuff has suffered of late. Only one of the bands is totally active. I don't know how I did all that stuff, but I know I can't do it now. I haven't rebuilt an amp for a year, which kind of bums me out.

But, I've also focused more on my writing and tried to not let anything get in its way. I have a lot of books I want to do before I die. Writing, along with Gayle and my friends, what I need to find time for. You could live 100 years and still not get to see the people you love enough. I doubt I'll be on my deathbed someday wishing I'd rebuilt one more amp, you know? Someone else can rebuild amps for a while, I guess. There are plenty of people who are better at it, anyway.

You've talked a lot about Gayle, your partner, is she your first reader?

Sometimes. When she isn't buried in student papers, she's the first. She's a great reader. When she's busy, there are a few writer friends of mine and we read each other's work. But if she's not the first, she one of the five people who I send work to. When she can, she always reads a story before it leaves the house. And with a novel, I won't send it to my agent until she's had a look. I think it might be pretty rare for your partner to be a real editor. She's very honest and she doesn't just say, "oh it's wonderful, you're so brilliant." She's a real reader—critical in the best ways. Rigorous. Supportive. Incredibly smart.

As far as talking about her a lot…well, Gayle warrants a lot of talking about. She is pretty fabulous.

You have a story being published in Penthouse, what's that about? How did you go about getting it in there?

It was a memoir excerpt about my cock piercing. My friend Steve Almond read it and suggested one editor at Playboy and one at Penthouse. Penthouse took it. They paid more for that 4 page piece than I've been paid for two of my books combined. Apparently, I should be writing about my cock more often. If I were more of a Capitalist, you might see nothing but cock from me for years.

Who are your favorite writers on your bookshelf? Anyone new that we should watch out for?

This is super tough, and I'm going to dance around it a bit. I hope you'll forgive me. I would love to name a bunch of deserving people and hope that your audience became their audience. But I know SO many great writers and many of them are very close friends of mine. And if I tried to give you a list of the writers who I admire from my generation/my contemporaries, it would be ridiculously long, and I would still, inevitably, accidentally forget someone (or a few people), and feel like absolute shit about it.

I will mention two who are friends, but I'll mention them because they are not exactly my contemporaries. Also, while they are good friends, they were, at first, mentors to me. Probably, in many ways, my two biggest teachers and influences and just fabulous writers: Francois Camoin and Darrell Spencer.

Francois, I got to study with in my MFA program. In fact, he's the reason I ended up getting the degree. I pretty much was thinking about dropping out, then I heard him read the story "Marty" from his incredible collection LIKE LOVE, BUT NOT EXACTLY. I'd had some fine teachers, but hearing Francois read was the first time I'd ever heard someone who wrote stories like I wanted, desperately, to write them, but couldn't for the life of me do at the time. At Vermont College, where I got my MFA, there was a system where the students list the mentor they want to work with the most, and then the second most, and so on, and you had to list five. It was weighted to seniority. I met/heard Francois when I had three terms to go. I picked him first. I didn't get him. I figured, the next time, I'd have only two terms left, and I had a better chance to get him. And you were allowed to work with the same mentor two terms in a row, so I was hoping to work with him the whole final year. Again, I didn't get him.

By then, we were friends. Also, by then, I'd read every word he'd ever published and was getting pretty pissed off at whoever assigned mentors. At that point, I had been there too long to drop out (though I had thought about it a lot, but I was damn well sure I was going to get to work with this guy)...I was pot-committed, in poker terms. I also figured they HAD to give me my first choice for my last term. Or else blood would be spilled in the program director's office and no one there would ever read in poet voice again, if I didn't get Francois.

And then Darrell Spencer, who I never studied with, but his stories taught me a lot about writing, and then we became friends and he's amazing. An afternoon hanging and talking casually with Spence can teach you more about writing that a semester long course with many people.

Those are two writers who should be much more widely read. **Can you tell us about The Cost of Living? When should we**

expect it?

It's a novel that takes place over 30 years (though not chronologically) in the life of the narrator—whose father killed a man when he was 13 and whose mother left the same year and committed suicide when he was 17. So, he's got some issues. I think it's my best book. I could be wrong, but this one got closer to what I'm trying to do than any of them so far. I'm doing the final edits now.

It's coming out on Other Voices (OV) Books, who are associated with Dzanc, and I'm happy to get to work with them. Especially working with OV Books editor Gina Frangello. She's a great writer, as well, and the best editor I've ever had. And I've been lucky with editors. But, she's in another league.

It's coming out in Fall, 2012. Unless those End Times bastards are right.

I see you interviewed yourself on thenervous breakdown.com. What's it like to be such an incredibly attractive writer—maybe the world's sexiest author?

Ha! It's going pretty well.

I saw you're writing a book on writing, how's that going, why did you feel you wanted to write it?

I think I started it for teaching. So I could have chapters on issues that come up so often in student manuscripts, and I thought I wouldn't have to keep saying it over and over, with every new group I get to work with. I could just say, "You're withholding information. That's an issue. Look at page 42, where it explains why."

It's suffering a bit, because I have so many other writing projects I want to do. I'm hoping to find more time for it in the future.

What's the best piece of advice you've heard in writing? The worst?

The best? Read. And read like a writer. How you read, the quality of what you read, and the amount that you read goes a

VERY long way to determining how far you may go as a writer. And work your ass off and expect two careers. One that pays for the writing, and the writing

The worst? Well, I won't name names, tempting as it may be, but this guy was the absolute worst guest-writer we have EVER had at UCR/Palm Desert, where I teach. A moronic cow-fucker of an idiot. After reading an astoundingly shitty story, he told the students he never revised (as if that were not frighteningly evident), and neither should they. I don't mind if I hear bad advice. For better or worse, I've been at this a while and I do what I do and I listen to good advice to improve. But after doing this for over 24 years, I can spot a moron.

But when someone says dumb-ass shit to my students? He's just lucky I'm a civil human being...or a chickenshit coward. Either way, someone should have gone on-stage and stapled the bottom of his tongue to his forehead.

Of course, after his terrible advice, what did he do? Went out on the University's dime and ordered the most expensive thing on the menu. The first smart thing he'd done all night.

How important is your education in regards to your writing?

My "degree" is not very important to my writing at all. But my education—which continues, for all of us (I hope) until we die—is essential to my writing. And my life. I can't imagine not thinking of every day, of every book, of every song, and so on, a chance to know more, feel more and get fresh ideas and influences for my work.

So, the work I did as a student in a degree-granting institution? That was very important, because I was learning and I was being mentored at a time that I really needed to understand how this craft and life worked.

But, my education keeps going. I learn from my friends—from their books and from our conversations and from their notes on my manuscripts. I learn from writers I'll never meet.

I've gotten a bonus education on my new novel (THE COST OF LIVING, due Spring, 2013, OV Books), getting to work with my friend and editor Gina Frangello (also a great writer, whose A LIFE IN MEN is coming on Algonquin in Fall, 2013). She's pushed me where I needed it. She's made me a better writer because she had something to teach me, and I had enough trust in her to learn.

You're always learning with writing. It's one of the beautiful things about the gig. And, hopefully, it teaches me that I should always be learning in life. We're always—in life—apprentices. The best read person on the planet hasn't read very much at all, considering what's out there. There's always more to learn

How do you know when a book is "finished?"

On this one, I'm going with: When Gina says so.

What are your thoughts on basing your characters on real people?

It's odd…I never do this. Not as a one-to-one correspondence, at any rate. Characters may have certain tics and qualities of people from my life, but I have never based a character on a specific person. I know writers who do it. It makes sense, in theory, to me. But it never happens when I write. My characters seem to come from somewhere else. And, again…they have attributes of tons of people I've known. But I, for some reason, never base characters on people.

What are three mistakes you made as a beginning writer?

Only three?

Well, first, I was terrible about sending the work out. I liked (well…liked is a complex word when it comes to writing…but I was obsessed, maybe is better) the writing part of the deal. I hated sending work out and doing what felt like…well, paperwork. And organization. And shit I'm not good at. But, at some point I realized that if I was going to take that kind of time and effort to create the work, and if I wanted people to read it— well, it was a necessary part of the deal to try to hustle to get the work to people.

Paradoxically, I was FAR too concerned with getting my work published early in my career when I should have been more concerned with becoming a better and more original writer. To be involved in writing because you love the process was a healthier way of doing it for me—but I had to learn to come to that. Oddly, when I started caring about doing great work and not caring that much about publication, that's when I started getting published. And I think the two are strangely related. For me, there was a real breakthrough with my writing when l realized this is what I do. And I wanted to do it as well as I could. And then, I realized that while l would like to be published, that would not determine whether or not I thought the work had merit. When my first story was accepted and then printed, I was published. Yet that story was the exact same story the day before it was accepted. I didn't get better the day of acceptance. I got better the days before that when I honored my craft.

Number three is a weird one: Always carry a notebook. For years, people told me to do this and for years, I figured if an idea was good, that idea would come back. I was wrong. Some great ideas only visit once. A writing notebook (and I don't mean a diary or journal…but a writing notebook of ideas and sections of work and overheard dialog and title ideas, and so on) has become essential to/for me.

What's next for Rob Roberge?

Well, once I see if it poisons my food-taster or not, I might have dinner. Thanks for the interview!

Thank you.

Goat

Bio

Rob Roberge is the author of the upcoming book of stories Working Backwards from the Worst Moment of My Life, the neo-noir novels More Than They Could Chew (Perennial Dark

Alley/Harper Collins, February 2005) and Drive (re-issue,Hollyridge Press, 2006). His stories have been featured in ZYZZYVA, Chelsea, Other Voices, Alaska Quarterly Review, and the "Ten Writers Worth Knowing Issue" of The Literary Review. His work has also been anthologized in Another City(City Lights, 2001), It's All Good (Manic D Press, 2004) and SANTI: Lives of the Modern Saints(Black Arrow Press, 2007). New work is scheduled to appear in OC Noir, part of the series that includes San Francisco Noir, LA Noir and Las Vegas Noir. Other new work is coming in PENTHOUSE.

Paul Tremblay

What comes to mind when you hear, "Mourning Goats?"

Oddly enough, I do not think of a farm animal that may or may not provide cheese depending upon its mood. I do not think of a farm animal that may or may not be in the service of Satan.

Instead, I instantly think of a literary blog/interview website!

With two novels, two short story collections, and two novellas published, you've seen many different sides of publishing, what do you think is the hardest to break in to? How did you do it?

Certainly, the big NYC publishers remain the most difficult to break into. How did I do it? Stubborn persistence, some talent, and a whole lot of luck, I guess. In 2003 I finished writing a quirky-comedy novel called PHOBIA. I managed to get pre-blurbs (for lack of a better term) from two amazingly talented and gracious writers: Poppy Z. Brite and Stewart O'Nan. Then I spent two plus years collecting over 200 agent rejects. Most of the rejects went something like: "This is funny and original, but we don't know who we can sell this to." I finally got my book on the desk of Stephen Barbara, pretty much by accident. I'd sent a query to another agent who no longer worked at the agency, but Stephen got the email and wanted to take a look. He understood the book, suggested some revisions (his suggestions were spot on) and he took me on as a client. Of course, we didn't sell the novel (the publishers said the same thing the other agents said: "Funny, original, but we don't know who we can sell this to"), but Stephen stuck with me. The sap.

I feel like being a writer isn't anywhere near as lonely as it used to be, since we now have blogs, social media, websites, etc. It's much easier to reach out to anyone. What do you like/dislike about this new accessibility?

The relatively new accessibility is my lifeline, frankly. So many of my good friends, and favorite writers and lit reviewers/bloggers are not geographically close to me. My being able to keep in touch with them so easily and frequently is not only a boon to my own work but to my sanity. Being able to have online corners and crannies where the struggle is shared is supremely important. At least it is, to me.

What I dislike is the exponentially expanding crush social media/information/sites that make it more difficult to figure out where a writer should be spending her/his time wisely. I dislike the glut of self-proclaimed genre experts (any genre, pick a genre) some of whom do more harm than good, in terms of their disseminating wrong or biased information (in regards to what's happening in the genre(s)). Don't get me wrong, with book coverage all but disappearing from print media outlets, book bloggers/reviewers are vital in filling that void. I guess what I'm saying is I wish more of the online folk were less interested in star f*cking, less interested in personal agendas, and were more interested in promoting diverse, healthy, inclusive genres and literature in general.

You are an advisor for the Shirley Jackson awards, what does that entail?

A few years ago (and with the help of a whole slew of folks behind and in front of the scenes) F. Brett Cox, JoAnn Cox, John Langan, Sarah Langan, and myself established the awards with the blessing of the Shirley Jackson estate. For the first two years, I was a juror. Since leaving the jury, I've assisted the administrator (JoAnn) and also served as an advisor. An advisor simply keeps an eye and ear out for works that would potentially be a good fit for the award, and sends those should-read-work-X suggestions to the jurors.

Thank you for In The Mean Time, it was brilliant, do you think short stories are easier or harder than novels?

Thank you! They may be harder to do well. Still, it's hard for me to compare the forms, to compare writing a 70,000 word novel to a 6,000 word short story. They are, obviously, different beasts. My first attempts at novel writing were pretty flawed: I was a short story writer trying to write a novel. Which meant that most of my early attempts at novels were loose, plotless, and lacking some narrative drive. With The Little Sleep (and the novels after), I wrote a ten-page plot synopsis before writing the novel, which I've found tremendously helpful.

But now that I have a handful of novels under my belt, writing short stories are more of a challenge than they were pre-novels. A challenge, if nothing else, to keep the word counts manageable: i.e. out of the dreaded novelette/novella range.

You've said that you didn't start seriously writing until 2000, while relatively new to it all, you're doing great, how do you explain your success?

Well, thanks. The why of whatever success (your mileage may vary on the definition of that word) I've had breaks down in exact percentages:

- 62.3% the kind help from other editors/writers and in the early-early going, friends and family who were and are willing to read my stuff and offer feedback and criticism
- 10% chronically overactive imagination
- 11.1% pessimism and negativeness
- 0.3% talent
- 16.3% my own damn hard work.

Man, I hope that adds up to 100%.

I don't know. It's hard for me to think about. The questions at either end of the pole—"Why does my stuff get read?" and "Why doesn't my stuff get read/bought more?"—tend to scare/freak me out, so I try not to dwell on either for too long.

Being a writer and working in a high school...are you scared for the future of literature?

Communication? Language in general? LOL...

I'm not really concerned about the future of language/ communication as it's always been evolving/changing.

If by the future of literature you mean publishing, then yeah, I'm scared. Despite my previously claimed 11.1% of pessimism, I'm trying to remain positive that publishing will not continue to devolve into a Mad Max world where the mid-list completely disappears, where the only genre books published will be fad based and feature zombies or steampunk, where big names writers are the only writers selling books, and where good books are hopelessly lost in a sea of self-published ebooks.

When researching, I kept reading about *Phobia*, can you tell us about it, and, what's happening with it?

PHOBIA is about Cam Cleeves, a neurotic dude with a whole host of odd fears: including the fear of the inability to complete simple tasks. Think Confederacy of Dunces in Boston.

Nothing is happening with it. It's in the trunk. Maybe some day, it'll get out there. But I'm not in a rush. It did it's job for me, as far as I'm concerned.

You are working on a Young Adult novel with fellow Mourning Goats interviewee, Stephen Graham Jones, what has that been like?

Stephen has not been callously trashing my contributions. He has not compared my writing to the inchoate scratching of a syphilitic Aye Aye. He has not issued any sort of threats, mocking or otherwise, should I fail to live up to his lofty standards. He certainly has not promised to cut off my fingers, in sections, one knuckle at a time, for every typo and grammatical mistake I might make in our manuscript.

*Sliding note under the door. HELP ME is written in old ketchup, at least you hope it's old

ketchup...*

Of course, I kid. It has been and continues to be an honor working with Stephen. He's been one of my favorite writers for years, and now, he's a cherished friend who will never beat me in basketball.

What's your favorite part about teaching? Also, would you consider teaching fiction?

Summer!

Well. I suppose I do enjoy working with kids. I enjoy teaching/telling people something they don't know. I like being part of that discovery: the discovery of some new nugget of truth. It's almost like writing in a way. A writer's job should be to tell the truth as how they see it.

I've had a few opportunities to teach writing workshops and they were a blast. I would definitely consider teaching a writing class. But at the same time, I'd be terrified of being exposed as a fraud.

What were the biggest differences you saw at the publishing houses?

At Holt I've had multiple editors, publicists, marketing conference calls, and other more sort of businessy (for lack of a better made up word) responsibilities and pressures. The smaller presses tend to be a count-on-one-hand number of people show. So bigger reach and power with the big house, a more personal touch with the smaller presses.

You have a master's degree in mathematics, most writers I know relate math to masochism, how were you drawn to it? Do you feel any connection between mathematics and writing?

As an unambitious kid, I stuck with math because I was good at it. And I more or less followed that path in college and grad school. Although, I only got into the UVM master's program because the dean of the math department fortuitously was moving his office in July of '93 and he found my lost application under his desk. Three days later I was in and had a teaching fellowship to boot.

I enjoy the logic and the order of math, particularly calculus. I enjoy the creativity that the higher levels of math require. I enjoy the funky symbols we get to use too. I don't think there is much of a writing connection to math, but perhaps I take an analytical approach to writing. I've never been able to just get a quick rough draft out and then chisel away at the mess until the final product appears. I plod ahead one sentence at a time, revising as I go, and I always write in order (by in order, I don't mean every story I write is linear, far from it. I just always start at what I think is the beginning of the particular story I'm writing and sally forth until I type the end, wherever that end might be).

The End. (Er, but only the end of the answer to that question!)

I just read that the New York Times is going to have an e-book top-seller list starting next year. Do you think this is necessary? Are e-readers a different breed than book readers?

I don't know if it's necessary (is anything necessary?), but it'll be interesting to see if the list mirrors the hardcopy best sellers list. I'm not sure we can conclude much about an entire group of people like that (e-readers). I guess if nothing else we can conclude they can afford to buy a relatively expensive electronic e-reading device of some kind (phone, computer, or separate device). I do find myself annoyed with the people who give books one star reviews because the kindle price is too high for their liking; espousing a lame-brained rationale of "oh the authors could stop this if they really wanted to." Because yes, that's how publishing works.

The Little Sleep and No Sleep Till Wonderland are your two published novels can you tell us anything about the third novel, Sleep at the End of the World? The title tells me that it might be true trilogy ender.

Well, it's a novel that might not ever happen. I'm currently not contracted to write a third Genevich novel, and I'm not working on it now. If I were to write a third, that would be the title and it would be the last.

You have a very eclectic style, who are some of your biggest influences? Are you reading anything now that you want our readers to know about?

I like to think I have a lot of influences, that everything I read influences me in some way. Writers I continue go back to for inspiration include Kurt Vonnegut, Aimee Bender, Stephen King, Stewart O'Nan, Chuck Palahniuk, and Jim Shepard.

Favorite books from 2010 that folks should read: Craig Davidson's Sarah Court, Aimee Bender's The Peculiar Sadness of Lemon Cake, and Laird Barron's Occultation.

In your Velvet interview, I love that you said, "when the writing is going good, I'm writing scared." Can you explain this a little more? Do you feel this often?

I'm scared that I'm not serving the story correctly, that I'm screwing up the plot or character or voice up. I'm scared that I'll have nothing important to say. And I write scared that no one will like it, or worse than no one liking it: it'll be met with apathy. A reader giving a shrug.

I feel this way whenever I'm writing fiction.

Do you write every day? Specific times? What does a normal day look like to Paul Tremblay?

Lately, I've fallen into doing most of my writing at night. But I still try and get stuff done at school if I have a free period. In the spring, when my school schedule calms down a bit, I can get more stuff done at school. Otherwise, it's at night, after the kids go to bed. I don't sleep enough.

You've started a "mainstream lit novel," can you tell us anything about it or do you keep that a secret until you've completed it?

Yeah, I don't want to really say anything about it. I've written a brief summary, and I'm afraid that if I say anything, then I'd be honor-bound to write it. I haven't decided if I'm going to go for it yet.

And I'm afraid if I talk about it here, Stephen will break my toes for admitting that I'm not solely working on our YA novel all hours of the day.

If you could go back and give yourself one piece of advice

before undertaking the writing of your first novel, what would it be?

Do you mean my first attempt at a novel? Or my first sold novel? My first sold novel is really like my 4.5th novel.

For The Little Sleep I'd tell myself to add zombies and/or sparkly vampires.

For my first ever attempt at a novel: I'd tell myself to relax and that it was okay to screw up, even okay to fail. Then I would've told that handsome bastard to write a plot outline/synopsis before sitting down to write the novel.

Other than the YA novel with Stephen Graham Jones and the mainstream lit novel, what else are you working on now?

Besides anything else I might've mentioned above, I'm co-editing with John Langan a reprint anthology called CREATURE! Thirty Years of Monster Stories. No werewolves, vampires, or zombies. Monsters.

John has yet to threaten my lovely fingers and toes like Stephen has. Give him time....

How important is your education in regards to your writing?

My educational background is different than most writers, I think. I got a Master's degree in mathematics and didn't start messing around with writing until after I got my first math teaching job. That said, an English class I took senior year in college as a part of my Humanities major, was very much influential. The course introduced me to Joyce Carol Oates for one, and the short fiction of hers led me to falling in love with reading.

My lack of formal training in writing is on one hand a source of pride, though a bit delusional at that: the idea that I'm self-taught. Of course, I have been trained in writing, just not in a classroom setting thanks to all the wonderful authors and editors that have helped me along the way. More times than not, though, I lean toward being self-conscious about my lack of educational background in English/writing, and how I came to be a writer later in the game than most. My self-esteem issues with that lack tends to drive and motivate me, though: it just means I have to work that much harder.

What are your thoughts on basing your characters on real people?

I base characters on real life people all the time. Family members, friends, enemies, people in the news; I steal from everyone. So should every writer. One of the aspects of writing that I enjoy is taking these pieces of real life people, mixing and matching, putting the pieces through my authorial centrifuge, and then putting the Frankenstiened character amalgams to work to serve the story. How's that for a jumble of mixed metaphors?

What are three mistakes you made as a beginning writer?

If only there were three...

1. Taking rejection and criticism personally. That's not to say rejection and criticism doesn't sting, it does. One little trick I use is to give myself a 24 hour cool-down period, where I won't respond to edits. I let myself grouse and bemoan for a day. Then, usually, I'm more able to be rational, to determine the merit of the suggested edits. Or, in the case of a rejection, I'm better able to move on and try the next market.

2. Don't obsess over the success of other writers. Show me a writer who hasn't at one point in their careers been jealous or pissed off by the successes of another hack...I mean...another writer. Okay, fine, you don't have to show me, but the point is, jealousy is natural. Just don't wallow in it. Burning too much of your mental energies on what other people have achieved won't help you. Instead, channel those mental energies into your doing your own thing.

3. Don't use goat's blood to write that horror story. Man, what a mess that was.

Thank you,

Goat

Bio

Paul Tremblay is the author of the novels The Little Sleep, No Sleep Till Wonderland (both Henry Holt), and the forthcoming Swallowing a Donkey's Eye. He is also the author of the short story collection In The Mean Time. His essays and short fiction have appeared in The Los Angeles Times, FiveChapters.com, and Best American Fantasy 3. He has co-edited four anthologies, including Creatures: Thirty Years of Monsters, and he is also the president of the board of directors for the Shirley Jackson Awards. www.paultremblay.net

John Langan

What comes to mind when you hear, "Mourning Goats?"

A small herd of goats—maybe five or six—gathered near the grassy top of a modest mountain. Their coats are almost comically long; their horns, undersized; the expression on their faces one of disaffection—indeed, they look like a talented child's approximation of a goat. At the very summit of the mountain, a grey stone box, its surface cracked, the cracks seemed with hardy lichen, rests. The goats range nearer and farther from the box, but there is a certain distance they will not venture any closer to it, just as there is another distance they will not stray any further. Ask one of the men or women who live in the village at the foot of the mountain about these animals, the stone box, and he or she will tell you that these are the Mourning Goats. The man or woman will not contradict you when you state that their mourning must be connected to the box, but when you try to explore the matter further, ask if the box is a tomb, or a monument, or maybe an altar, he or she will refuse to answer you. It is not good to speak of such things, you will be told, and that is all you will be told. If you insist on hiking the mountain to examine the goats and their charge, you will see a look of panic flash across the face of the man or woman with whom you are speaking, but he or she will not stop you.

You're a teacher at SUNY New Paltz, a story writer, novelist, non-fiction writer, father, husband, and practice karate— that was tiring just to type out; how do you do it?

Well, I had to drop karate because my knees couldn't take it, anymore, and I only teach part-time at SUNY New Paltz, which helps my schedule (if not my bank account). Aside from that, it's a balancing act. I suppose it's gotten a little easier in the last couple of years, as my son has reached school age, but even so, it's a matter of prioritizing. As just one example: I used to try to do a lot more non-fiction—book reviews, especially—than I do now; that's because I realized the number of book reviews I was writing was taking too much time away from my fiction writing, which was what I most wanted to focus on. Life is fluid, so you have to be prepared to accommodate that.

How has working with Night Shade Books been? Do you see a lot of differences when working with different publishers as well as different genres of writing?

All things considered, I've been very fortunate in the publishers I've worked with. Prime, who did my collection, Mr. Gaunt and other Uneasy Encounters, made sure that the book went out to a huge number of review outlets, as a result of which, I received reviews from publications such asThe San Francisco Chronicle, The L.A. Times, and The Washington Post. Night Shade took a novel, House of Windows, that the genre folks thought was too literary and the literary folks thought was too genre, and produced a lovely book. When the hardcover didn't sell as well as they wanted, they went back to the drawing board and redesigned the trade paperback edition, which has done somewhat better.

Having worked with only two publishers, I'm not sure I'm qualified to make any kind of broad statement about publishing. In terms of working in different genres, the only other genre in which I've published has been the non-fiction/academic one, and there, I've been very fortunate in terms of finding a number of editors who have been receptive to what I've wanted to write about.

As an academic, what are your thoughts on teaching writing, and learning how to write: do you believe it's something that is taught, something that is just there, or something else?

I guess I'd have to say, "Yes." There's no denying that some people have that facility with language and storytelling that we stuff under the name talent. At the same time, no matter that raw ability, there's always more that can be done to refine it, not to mention, to develop the discipline required to sit down at the page every day until the story or poem is done.

A lot of this, I'm absolutely certain, has to do with how much and how well you've read. We learn through imitation, and if you have that nascent ability with language and storytelling (which I suspect is far more widespread than we might think), then you want to allow yourself the maximum number of examples to learn from. I know that writing workshops are very popular and certainly, they can be useful, but I'd suggest that it may be as, if not more, useful for a beginning writer to engage in a program of intensive reading, take a year or two and just soak yourself in the written word.

I feel like most of my favorite authors have had very interesting jobs, any you'd like to share? Do you think that these experiences have shaped the way your writing has gone? Why?

My job experiences have been a tad less colorful: aside from teaching since the mid-nineties, the majority of my past work-experience has been in eye-care: in my younger years, I worked for both optometrists and ophthalmologists. These were useful jobs, not because of anything to do with their specialty so much as because they brought me into contact with a wide variety of people, both in terms of my co-workers and the patients who came into the different offices. (Now that I think about it, teaching at a state university these past years has done the same thing). It's very useful for a writer to be exposed to as wide a range of people as is possible, since they are the raw material from which you will make your art. That and stories: the more people you meet, the more stories you hear, and what writer doesn't love stories?

The first short story you had published, "On Skua Island," was an 11 or 12 thousand word piece, which is quite long for a short story. How did you get it in to the Magazine of Fantasy and Science Fiction? What did it feel like to have such a big piece taken by such a big magazine so early?

Yes, "On Skua Island" falls under that nebulous heading known as "novelette:" too long for a short story, too short for a novella. I submitted it to F&SF because they were one of the few magazines willing to look at such long fiction unsolicited. (They still are). I sent it to them the old-fashioned way, via snail-mail, and was astonished to receive a check and contract from Gordon Van Gelder within about a month. I can still remember standing at the mailbox at the end of the driveway in my bathrobe, tearing open the envelope. As I'm sure you can imagine, it was a big boost to the ego of a fledgling horror writer to have a story accepted by the magazine that had published Stephen King. In addition, Gordon did a good deal to promote the story in the months leading up to its publication. It was a little overwhelming; I had started at the top, not expecting to succeed there, and suddenly, I had and there I was. It's the reason I advise beginning writers to aim for the heights: the worst that can happen is that you receive a rejection letter, the best is that you find yourself in a position of tremendous advantage.

You've been teaching reading and writing for over fifteen years. What's your favorite part, least favorite part?

I've loved the diversity of students teaching at a public university has brought me into contact with, and I've loved having the chance to expose them to a wide variety of literary texts. As a writer, there's no surer way to make sure you maintain contact with the classics than by teaching them on a regular basis. I think I've benefited from returning to texts like "A Good Man Is Hard To Find" and Heart of Darkness and The Turn of the Screw as many times as my teaching has made me.

What don't I like? Grading can be a bit of a drag, especially when you have a student who hasn't taken the assignment seriously, and so has wasted their time and yours.

In one interview you discussed that comics are slowly moving in to academia; do you see this as a shift in what is considered literary?

Well, to split hairs, I see this as a shift in what modes of writing are considered worthy of academic attention; from what I've been able to tell, however, there hasn't been much of a shift in the topics that are considered suitable for academic notice. What I mean is, a comic such as Art Spiegelman's Maus, which addresses the Holocaust and the vexed relationship between a father and son, treats subjects that are already considered literary; while a comic such as Eric Powell's The Goon, which engages the history of pulp fiction conventions in a raucous and innovative fashion, is by and large still deemed beyond the pale.

What's it like being a judge for the Shirley Jackson Awards? What does being a judge entail?

Being a juror for the first three years of the Shirley Jackson award was a great privilege. No surprise, the job entailed a lot of reading, not just the books that publishers would mail you, but whatever you could seek out that might qualify. I was quite pleased with the shortlists we arrived at: if you wanted a cross-section of some of the best horror and dark fiction being written today, you could do a lot worse than use those lists as a guide.

You're co-editing a monster anthology called Creatures with another Mourning Goat interviewee, Paul Tremblay. What's it like working with him; are you working on anything with any other authors right now?

Paul has been a real pleasure to work with; he's uber-organized, conscientious, and professional. To the extent that Creatures succeeds, it's because of the weeks and weeks of hard work that he's put into it. At some point in the future, Paul and I are supposed to collaborate on what's going to be a terrific short story or novelette; Laird Barron and I are also kicking around the idea of doing a story together.

In one of your Facebook posts you wrote that your son, David, was waiting to read the beginning of his first chapter book. Was this a book he wrote, or a book he wanted to read to you? Either way, what are your thoughts on your kids getting

into the literary world?

This was a book that David wanted to read to my wife and I; the title escapes me, now, but it had something to do with the labyrinth. Since that time, though, he has begun work on his own book, The Dictionary of Monsters. Yes, apples, trees, and all that. My older son, Nick, has flirted with film-making at various points in his life; in fact, he was the one who shot and edited the trailer for my first novel, House of Windows. He's also written several screenplays for a cartoon series that would be great, if only he could find someone to take an interest in it.

On the one hand, there's no denying the excitement you feel as a parent when your kid is doing what you do; there's a kind of validation to it that is hard to describe and very gratifying. On the other hand, kids have to find their own identities, which means that they're likely going to wind up doing something different than what you do, the same way you chose to do something different from what your parents did. That said, there's no doubt that, whatever my boys choose to do, a facility with reading and writing can only help them.

You're a two-time International Horror Guild Award finalist for short fiction and Mr. Gaunt and Other Uneasy Encounters was nominated for the 2009 Bram Stoker Award. Do you find short fiction easier than novels? Which is your favorite medium to write and why?

Well, short fiction can provide more immediate gratification (relatively speaking) than novel-length projects, both in terms of the speed with which you can finish it and in which it can be published. Right from the start, though, my work tended towards the longer end of the spectrum, long-novelette/short novella, so moving up to the novel felt like more of a natural progression than it might have had I been writing short short stories. (Indeed, writing shorter stuff is something I'm still working on). At this point, I haven't completed enough novels to compare writing them to writing stories of any length with any kind of certainty, but I'm a sucker for a good novella. At about a hundred pages, you have the freedom to develop your characters and the situation confronting them in some depth, but you haven't completely sacrificed the concision of effect.

I saw that you went to World of Fantasy last year: what did you think of it? Do you think that these kinds of events are important to aspiring writers?

Since I was completely left off the programming, an omission that wasn't confirmed until I was standing in the convention hotel, trying to find my name somewhere on the schedule, this past World Fantasy was not among the best I've ever attended. I suppose that extra free time did allow to me to spend a little more time with friends I don't get to see that often, such as Nick Mamatas, which was good, and to make the acquaintance of a number of writers I knew only through their work, such as Gary Braunbeck, which was also nice.

The usefulness of these events depends, I think, on the individual writer. I didn't attend my first convention until I'd had three stories published in F&SF, two of which, as you've noted, had been nominated for an award. As a result, I received a very kind reception from the people I talked to, and found the convention experience, on the whole, an encouraging one. Had I gone before I had anything published, I'm not sure how I would have felt. Based on my observations, the genre community tends to be fairly welcoming; however, the younger me, who was even more prone to self-doubt than the older me, might very well have been overwhelmed by meeting real writers who were actually writing, and that might have done me more harm than good.

Do you think that making a good horror is about making a monster that you detest as well as sympathize with?

I think good horror is more about making characters with whom the reader will sympathize. A good monster is nice, but if those it threatens aren't compelling, then you get a kind of slaughter-fantasy that doesn't seem particularly interesting to me. That said, a good monster combined with good characters is pretty hard to beat.

You have a facebook page, blog, and twitter account; do you think that social media is important for literature, authors, and the future of the written word?

With a few, Thomas Pynchonesque exceptions, I don't think you can avoid social media at this point. Some writers, such as Jeff Vandermeer, have employed it brilliantly to their careers' advantages; I would not lump myself in with them. I'm not sure what the implications of social media will be for the future of the written word; to be honest, from what I've seen, it strikes me as a danger to a lot of writers, a great time-suck into which a lot of the energy that should be going to your fiction gets drained. There's also the danger in presuming that, because you have a certain number of facebook friends, or twitter followers, or what have you, you have achieved something, that whatever flame wars you've spearheaded count for something in your life as a writer. I'm all for people expressing themselves online, and I've no doubt a number of worthy conversations have happened there, but fiction writers write fiction. That's what they do. If you're spending all your time online, you may be doing a lot of things, but writing fiction is not one of them.

Your 10 year anniversary is coming up this year (congratulations!): is your wife your first reader and what's it like being married to a fellow academic?

Thanks! In many ways, it's hard to believe it's been that length of time. My wife used to be my first reader—actually, it would be more accurate to say she was my first listener: once I'd written one or two thousand words, I would read it to her, and she would tell me what she thought. And she was honest, ruthlessly so. My wife understands narrative mechanics in a more deep and profound way than anyone else I've ever met; I probably learned more from the years we spent doing that than I had in all my writing classes up to then. After our son was born, though, it became much more difficult to maintain that kind of process, and it fell by the wayside; though I still have thoughts of returning to it, someday.

Certainly, the nice thing about being married to a fellow academic is that there's a level of understanding between the two of us that is deep and immediate; we don't have to explain or justify things to one another the way we might if we worked very different jobs. At the same time, our areas of study are sufficiently different for us to preserve some sense of our own identities.

What are some of the most recent things you've read— shorts, novels, whatever—that have knocked your socks off?

This year, I shied away from compiling any kind of "year's best" list because I'm aware that there's a great deal of fiction that I either haven't read yet or that's slipped completely underneath my radar. That admission out of the way, the books published this past year that absolutely blew my doors in were Laird Barron's Occultation and Paul Tremblay's In the Mean Time, both collections of short fiction.

With his first book, The Imago Sequence (2007), Laird seemed to arrive on the horror scene fully-formed, his plots a demonstration of the continuing vitality of what I guess you could call the cosmic horror tradition, his language a decanting of Cormac McCarthy, Wallace Stevens, and Roger Zelazny. Occultation consolidates the gains of the previous book while expanding Laird's range; I'm especially fond of his long stories, "The Broadsword" and "Mysterium Tremendum," but there isn't a clunker in the bunch. Laird could stop writing today and the achievement of his first two books would be sufficient to rank him with the major horror writers of the last century.

Paul's first collection, Compositions for the Young and Old (2004, rev. 2005), marked him as a writer to watch, and the stories he's published since that time have shown a learning curve so steep it's pretty much vertical. In the last half a dozen, seven years, he's written stories such as "There's No Light Between Floors" and "It's Against the Law to Feed the Ducks" and "The Teacher" that have vaulted him to the forefront of contemporary horror writers. For a good couple of years, now, I've been saying that when Paul's next collection came out, it was going to be a major event, and there's no other way to describe In the Mean Time.

I'd also like to mention a collection I'm in the middle of, Livia Llewellyn's Engines of Desire, which is new this year. Livia's stories are a fierce, uncompromising blend of the erotic and the horrifying, and her book is not to be missed.

As I'm sure you know, a lot of our readers are aspiring young writers. What piece of advice do you wish you received when you started putting words down?

That's a tough one. I think it would have been something like, "Read widely and well, but trust the things you love to be sufficient for your ambitions."

What does your writing routine look like, every day, when the thought hits, morning, night?

I have a small office in the northeast corner of our house, and that's my preferred place to work. When I'm engaged in writing a new story or working on a novel, I sit at my desk and do my best to produce at least a new page every day. Over the last couple of years, I've found myself more able to write in other locations—in my class, when my students are critiquing one another's work, or at the café at the base of the building that contains my office—so if I have a decent block of time, I'll try to usc it to continue with whatever I'm working on.

You're currently working on your second short story collection and your second novel. How are things going? What can you tell us about either/both?

The collection is currently making the rounds at a number of different publishers. It's called Technicolor and Other

Revelations, and includes eight stories, seven of which have been printed in places like John Joseph Adams's first Living Dead anthology and Ellen Datlow's Poe anthology, and one of which is brand new. I suppose these stories continue the trend I began in my first collection, which is to say, revisiting the central archetypes of horror narrative and seeing what I can do with them.

My second novel has the working title of The Fisherman, and I'm probably about sixty percent done with it. It's about a fishing trip to a haunted river. I hope to have it in to my agent come the beginning of summer.

How important is your education to your writing?

It's been very important; although, at the risk of sounding overly precious and/or pretentious, I want to say that I've benefitted from my educations. My formal education, earning first my BA, then my MA, and presently, my Ph.D., in English Literature has introduced me to both the major movers and shakers of the last few thousand years of literary endeavor, and lesser-known but no less valuable writers. It's also taught me a variety of ways to approach and appreciate those figures and what they've done, and given me venues in which I could discuss them with other, like-minded individuals. At the same time, though, I've been educating myself in the traditions of popular literature which have spoken to me and in which I've wished to work, Gothic horror, in particular, but also the major strains of science fiction and fantasy, mystery/crime fiction, and comic books. It goes without saying, there's been no small amount of bleed over from one strand of education to the other, with the techniques of analysis I've learned in the classroom coming in useful for parsing the works of Peter Straub or Samuel Delany; while the works of writers such as James Cain or Dashiell Hammett have helped to flesh out my understanding of what was happening during Modernism. In all instances, it's been grist for the mill of my development as a writer. Do I really have to say that, if you want to write, you have to read? Yes, you have to write, too, but if you haven't read widely and well, you're like an athlete coming to play a game whose rules and traditions s/he knows only by a poorly-xeroxed handout. I sometimes think that, instead of spending so much time in this writing workshop or that, an aspiring writer would do better to throw her/himself into a reading workshop.

For the sake of completeness, I suppose I should add that the time I've spent on college campuses has been important to me in terms of providing me a good deal of the setting and material for my fiction. There really are eight million stories in the naked campus.

How do you know when a book or story is finished?

Who was it that said no book is ever finished, only abandoned? For me, at least, there's some truth to that statement. I'm not sure there's anything I've published that I couldn't have put through one more round of revisions, and one more after that, and another...and so on, until I'd devoted my life to perfecting a single story. There's a certain obsessive, even monkish quality to that quest that I find appealing, the conceit of playing Harold Brodkey and spending almost all of your professional life at work on one piece of fiction. I'm absolutely a believer in the importance of revision, of not rushing a piece to completion, and yet, this kind of fetishizing of craft can become self-defeating; I'm reminded of that character in Conrad's The Secret Agent who's trying to create the perfect detonator. When he does, it takes him with it. I find it useful to remember Henry James's dictum that genius does *not* require perfection. There comes a time in the life of every piece of narrative when it's time for the writer to let it go and move onto what's next. Thus far, I've found that my sense of when that is has varied from piece to piece. I think it has something to do with my feeling that the story in question is hanging together as a whole, at the level of character and plot, of language and imagery, of theme and allusion. It doesn't hurt if it has a killer ending, too.

What are your thoughts on basing your characters on real people?

In one way, I think it's inevitable, since your inventions, however extravagant, are always going to be based in your experience. The problem, of course, is when your awareness of those connections hobbles your story, either because you have a strong emotional response to that person, and so idealize or demonize him/her, or because you confine your character's actions and decisions to your narrowest imagining of what that person might do. In each case, the writer's inability to allow the character to grow into what the story needs, which is to say, a complex actor capable of surprising choices, hinders her/his work. I suppose it could be rooted in an anxiety about what your best friend or mother will say when s/he realizes you've made him/her the protagonist of your story. In that case, though, you've stopped thinking like a writer and have put other concerns first. For the writer, what must come first, last, and in the middle is what will best serve the story at hand. I should note, though, that unless you tell them yourself or tip them off in some blatantly obvious way, most people will not recognize that they're the actors in your drama.

Thank you,

Goat

Bio

John Langan is the author of a novel, House of Windows (Night Shade 2009), and a collection of short stories, Mr. Gaunt and Other Uneasy Encounters (Prime 2008). With Paul Tremblay, he has co-edited Creatures: Thirty Years of Monster Stories (Prime 2011). His stories have appeared in The Magazine of Fantasy & Science Fiction, as well as anthologies including The Living Dead (Night Shade 2008), Poe (Solaris 2009), Supernatural Noir (Dark Horse 2011), Blood and Other Cravings (Tor 2011), and Ghosts by Gaslight (Harper Collins 2011). His next collection, Technicolor and Other Revelations, will be published in 2012 by Hippocampus Press. He lives in upstate New York with his wife and son.

Donald Ray Pollock

What do you think of when you hear the term, Mourning Goats?

I think of a man I use to work with at the paper mill. His name is Charley, but everyone called him "Goat" because he had a well-groomed van dyke beard. He used to come to work very hungover at times, which reminds me of the "mourning" aspect of your question.

You just sold your novel, The Devil All The Time, to Doubleday, so what can you tell us about it? (Published July 12th, 2011)

The Devil All The Time is set mostly in Ohio and West Virginia during the 1950's and 1960's. Picture a tough, upright young man, a pair of serial killers, a corrupt sheriff, dirty preachers, religion, lust, revenge, death, the often smudged line between good and evil, etc. The dust jacket art is fantastic; as my friend Chris Tusa said, it's sort of a cross between Faulkner and Orwell.

I heard about your story collection, Knockemstiff, from Chuck Palahnuik. Any idea how it got in his hands, and what it meant for the book?

Sure, the book was placed in Chuck's hands by my editor at Doubleday, Gerry Howard, who is also Chuck's editor. I think a lot of things in publishing work this way. Of course, having Chuck's endorsement helped the sales tremendously. He's a damn nice guy, that's all there is to it.

What was it like going back to school after 28 years? Do you think being a big reader made it any easier?

Well, I started attending college in 1988, which was, thank God, before computers began taking over (Did you know that scientists are now saying that they will be able to build a robot that's smarter than humans within thirty years? If that happens, we're screwed, though I guess it's inevitable that we will destroy ourselves, right?). Anyway, I probably did much better in school at age 35 than I ever would have at 19 or 20. For one thing, I was sober by then, I'd already been married a couple of times, and I had a lot of the horse-shit out of the way.

Being a big reader will help make just about anything easier. It's hard to believe there are people enrolled in college these days who have never read a book on their own. It would be nice if, instead of lowering the standards of college classes so that people who are practically illiterate can pass, we could create more jobs for our citizens who, let's face it, aren't cut out for higher education. Sorry, but I'm one of those people who believe that grades one through eight should be nothing but *lots* of reading, writing, and math, along with phys. ed. Get back to the basics and quit fucking with new-fangled approaches or state tests. Make it tougher on students, not easier. And figure out something to do with those who can't cut it or won't try. But then what do I know? I was a high school dropout.

You said in another interview that you write from around 6 am to 11 am; is that still how you work, or did things change when you started writing the novel?

Well, I worked mostly mornings on The Devil All The Time until the last four or five months, and then I switched to nights, from around 7 or 8 pm until 2-3 am. I like the idea of doing my work in the morning, of getting something done first thing so I don't have to fret about it all day, but I probably write a little better at night. Still, the main thing is to make the attempt every day.

It sounds like you're a voracious reader; anything recently that's blown your mind?

Believe me, I don't read that much. I try to read two books per week. I know that sounds like a lot to some people these days, but it's not, not if you want to be a writer anyway. Or anything else for that matter. I've got friends who read much more than I do. Think of all the hours the average citizen spends watching TV or playing video games or talking on their cell phone or handing their Facebook "commitments." Don't get me wrong, I can become as strung out on that junk as the next person, but it's not a good way to spend a major portion of your life (and I realize others would argue that reading isn't a good way either).

Except for Fred Venturini's novel, The Samaritan, the best fiction books I've read recently are all new story collections: From the Darkness Under Our Feet by Patrick Michael Finn, One Last Good Time by Michael Kardos and Volt by Alan Heathcock. Great non-fiction books I've read in the last couple of months include Gulag by Anne Applebaum, Fraser's Penguins by Fen Montaigne and King Leopold's Ghost by Adam Hochschild. I'm looking forward to reading the new memoirs by Mark Richards and Andre Dubus III.

Are you planning on focusing more on novels now that one is under the belt or do you think you'll go back and forth between novels and shorts?

I'm not sure yet. I have a new novel started (just barely), so that's pretty much all I'll be working on for next 18 months or so, and that's as far as I want to plan ahead. I'm not one of those people who can work on several different things at once.

In a lot of interviews, it sounds like you started writing because you had a mid-life crisis; do you think that's it, or do you think you just made the decision to go after something you knew you had in you?

Well, I think I just refer to that time as a "mid-life crisis" because I don't know what else to call it. But it wasn't like I was going to blow my brains out if I didn't change careers. If I'd waited, oh, just a few more months when I was going through that deal before I started writing, I would probably still be working at the paper mill and be happy with it.

Your story reminds me a lot of Craig Clevenger's; he wanted to be a writer, quit his job, and went for it. What do you wish

you would have known before you quit?

Nothing. If I had known some of the things I discovered later on—such as the difficulty of landing a decent teaching job, what such a job entails (hard work!) if you do it right, the cost of health insurance, etc.—there's a very good chance I would not have left the paper mill. I had a good job there.

You've said that you were 45 when you decided you wanted to learn to write. Do you think people learn how to write or are they born to write?

I definitely believe you can learn to write. Why not? Hell, you learn to be a plumber or drive a truck or be a lawyer, don't you? Granted, it takes longer to become a good writer than, say, a grill cook, but it's still a learned activity to a great degree. Certainly talent in involved, but it mostly comes down to hard work, like anything else. You can be the most talented writer in the world, but if you don't do the work, you might as well be whacking the heads off chickens in a processing plant.

One of my favorite pieces of advice that you give is that a person must learn to sit in the chair if he wants to be a writer. What's another big one for you?

You must read a lot if you really want to be a writer. If you don't love books and love to read, you'll never be a very good writer. And don't just read the type of stuff you like or aspire to write yourself. Read the classics, read poetry, read history. With the American library system, being ignorant or illiterate is inexcusable today, totally a matter of laziness and poor parenting and too much cable TV and "social networking." Texting your pal to tell him/her you're taking the trash out or just left the grocery store is not only insane behavior—at the very least either a sign of egomania or complete helplessness/co-dependency—but is time wasted. Those minutes add up. Do you want to go to your grave knowing that you spent a substantial chunk of your life tweeting?

With Knockemstiff, you did your first book tour—did you

like it? What would you like to see happen with The Devil All The Time as far as touring goes?

Even though I'm one of those people who has a hard time getting up in front of an audience and reading, I loved most of it. It's very hard for a shy person to stay stuck away in a room months or even years and then suddenly emerge and go out and read in front of a group. Still, it was a great experience, and I'm grateful for it. I met a lot of wonderful people. As for the tour for The Devil All The Time, the most I can hope for is that people like the book, and we sell a lot of copies.

How has the PEN/Robert Bingham Fellowship helped you finish your new book?

The PEN/Bingham did just what it's supposed to do—gave me the free time to work on a novel. Going to New York and receiving that award has to be up there in the six or seven best days of my life so far.

I have read that you wanted to teach. What made you go after that, and how has it been so far?

Though I'm probably shooting myself in the foot by admitting this, I have come to the conclusion in the last couple of years that I'm not a very capable teacher. To be good in the classroom, you have to at least *think* that you know what you're talking about, and I don't have that confidence. Perhaps it's because I started too late, I don't know. I don't think I'm bad with short gigs, like a week-long workshop or something like that, but I run out of new things to say after a few classes.

You have a website and a blog, but I didn't see a Facebook page. Did I miss it? What are your thoughts on social media these days?

Actually, I'm still trying to figure that out. I was on Facebook for a few months and then dropped off when it started taking up too much time and space in my head. I have a very addictive/compulsive personality, and I found myself messing with FB when I should have been writing (believe me, sometimes

I will do anything to keep from writing) or reading or exercising or anything else. Not only that, but I believe people need a certain degree of privacy and quiet time, whether they realize it or not. But now I'm back on FB, as of last week. Believe me, I understand that it's a great "marketing" tool, and also a great way to find people (and organize revolutions!). Still, I have to admit that I'm one of those dinosaurs who sometimes pines for the days of snail mail and typewriters and rotary phones.

I enjoyed reading your blog, but has the experience of quitting the mill, writing the book, going to school, and changing your life been all smiles? What were some of the struggles that you want to remember?

I really can't say I had any "struggles." I had a lot of rejections, and I spent a lot of time staring at the wall in the attic, but I'd be hesitant to call that sort of thing a struggle. Since I tend to compare my life with the lives of people who have it worse (not better), I see myself as very, very lucky. You have to understand that most of my "struggles" took place before I began writing, in the years before I got sober.

Drinking and writing go hand in hand, and you haven't had a sip since 1986. Do you think you'd be where you are today if you hadn't made the decision to quit?

If I hadn't stopped drinking in 1986, I would have been dead by 1990 or so. I still think about that, about how lucky I was to have that little moment of clarity one sick, hungover morning when so many people around me just kept on using until they died or ended up completely wasted.

You remind me of a darker Raymond Carver, maybe in the way you see the people that you write about. Was he a big influence and/or who is?

Of course, I read Carver's stories, and I think his spare prose style has been a big influence, but as far as subject matter/tone, etc., I've probably gotten the most from the Southern writers — Barry Hannah, Flannery O'Conner, William Gay, Tennessee

Williams, Larry Brown, Faulkner, Harry Crews. But right now my favorite fiction writers are J.F. Powers and Muriel Sparks and William Maxwell.

What do you think Ms. Herman, at Ohio State University, meant for your writing career?

As I've said many times, I'd probably still be working at the paper mill if it wasn't for Michelle. She published my first story in The Journal and encouraged me to apply for grad school. She's been great to me and many other students at OSU.

Knockemstiff had a rather high print run for a short story collection. How did that come about? Did it make you nervous at all?

I have no idea how they calculated the number of copies to print. Actually, I don't even recall how many copies were printed. The main thing I was concerned with was that they not lose any money on me. I figured if they didn't lose any money, well, maybe they would be willing to take another chance on me. The same with The Devil All The Time.

What does Don Pollock have planned for 2011?

I live a very quiet, small-town life for the most part. I get up and work a while, then try to get some exercise and read and that's about it. Last night I went to a high school basketball game; tonight I'll probably watch a movie; tomorrow morning I'll go to church (St. Paul's Episcopal Church in Chillicothe, Ohio) with my wife. Except for doing a book tour this summer, I'll probably just keep plugging away at the new novel.

How do you know when a book is finished?

When I'm absolutely sick of working on it. With both books I've finished, I really bore down the last 3 months or so, to the point where it was just cigarettes and caffeine and staying up all night. I guess my obsessive/compulsive stuff kicks in and I just ride it out. But I'm old and 12-15 weeks is all I can handle of a schedule like that.

Do you have a favorite part of being a published writer?

Being able to just stay home and write. I've been lucky and frugal enough to be able to do that the last 3 years or so.

Do you see the publishing changing with all the technological advances today? How? Are you excited about it?

Well, my first book came out just around four years ago, so a lot of that stuff was already starting to happen, I guess. I have a page on Facebook, for example, and also a web site, though I probably don't tend to them like I should. As for being excited, "sad" might be a better word. As I've said many times, I'm one of those people who long for the old days of rotary phones and snail mail and typewriters with ribbons. I tend to believe that technology is only a good thing up to a certain point and it seems as if we're about to go beyond that point.

Thank you,

Goat

Bio

Donald Ray Pollock grew up in Knockemstiff, Ohio, and dropped out of high school when he was seventeen. He worked at a paper mill in Chillicothe, Ohio, for thirty-two years before enrolling in the MFA program at Ohio State University. His first book, a collection of short stories entitled Knockemstiff, was awarded the PEN/Robert Bingham Fellowship in 2009. The Devil All the Time, his first novel, was listed by Publisher's Weekly as one of the ten best books of 2011.

Stephen Elliott

What comes to mind when you hear, "Mourning Goats?"

I think of that movie, The Men Who Stare at Goats. I never saw it.

In 2008, you started The Rumpus, what has it taught you about writing, life, etc.?

The main thing it taught me is the importance of community in relation to art. People, especially in the current, fragmented environment, want to be able to share the experience of art with others. I hadn't realized that before.

Also, with The Rumpus, you've started branching out with book clubs and daily emails, where do you see the website going?

Those are the two biggest things. The Daily Emails were supposed to just be links to interesting content but then I started adding my thoughts and eventually they became mini-essays, exercises in creative non-fiction, literary and very personal. People would sign up for the list and receive 2,000 word monologues on love and politics and everything else. About two months ago we finally changed the site so it reads "Sign up for The Daily Rumpus and receive overly personal emails" so at least now people have a better idea of what they're getting.

But the thing about the emails that was surprising to me is how fulfilling they are. I really enjoy writing them. For a long time I would feel guilty because I thought I should be working on a book. Now, when people ask what I'm working on I say email. It's the bulk of my creative activity, and I'm fine with that. It's kind of new and exciting, actually.

As for the book club when we had the idea to start a book club and charge $25 a month we thought we would have twenty members but right now we have about 540, 440 in the regular book club and 100 in the poetry book club. It's changed everything. It's the main thing funding The Rumpus which two people work on full-time (myself and Isaac Fitzgerald).

The book club makes me very hopeful about reading.

You have seven books so far, do you prefer fiction, non-fiction, or stories? I've read that you think non-fiction is harder because you can't embellish. Do you prefer to write in a specific genre or is there a love for all forms?

It's really just about the phase I'm in. Recently I've been missing fiction. There are ways in which the constraints of non-fiction can force you to be more creative, but it's more a mood. The important thing is to reach people, at least for me. To write something couldn't be found elsewhere. There's no point in writing a good book. There's lots of good books. There needs to be more to it than that, either that it's a great book or that it serves and represents and under-represented population.

I was a part of your Lending Library, for The Adderall Diaries, where did you come up with the idea, how do you think it turned out, and do you think you'll do it again?

The lending library turned out great. I was able to get 400 people to read The Adderall Diaries before it was released. It was a lot of work, bothering everybody to forward the book to the next reader, etc. I don't know if I'd do it again. I'm the type of person that only enjoys doing something once, then I look for different ways.

Most writers have a schedule that they try to keep while writing, and with you doing a daily newsletter for The Rumpus, and your personal life, how do you find time to write? What's a day in the life of Stephen Elliott look like?

The writing I do is for the daily email. That's pretty much all of it. I work on it until about eleven. The rest of the work day is maintaining The Rumpus, or other things.

Do you think that the publishing world is prospering from the digital revolution that's happening right now (everything from facebook, twitter, and myspace to e-readers, iPad, and

smart phones)?

I don't know. "Publishing world" is a slippery term. Some people are hurting. The writers don't need anybody. There'll always be writers. Literary writing has always been, and always will be, a labor of love. The larger publishing houses might die, and that doesn't bother me except I know some very nice people that work in those places. The majority of people who stay in publishing will do it for the love until they can't anymore.

You were a Stegner fellow, without an MFA, bravo! How did that happen and what are your thoughts on the teaching of writing?

Anybody can apply for a Stegner fellowship. I have a lecture I give on using your life in your writing. I think it's really helpful for writers. It's something I know about. I don't have much to say about teaching writing. I'm much better at lecturing than I am at leading a workshop. I hate reading students' writing, which is a jerk thing to say, but it's why I rarely teach workshops.

What do you think about book tours? You had your own way of doing it for The Adderall Diaries, can you tell us a little bit about that? I'm sure you experienced some pretty bizarre situations. Any list toppers you care to share?

My way was basically to say I would read in anyone's house if they promised to get at least 20 people to attend and would let me sleep on their couch. It was really fun, and draining, and when it was all over I kind of had a breakdown that I didn't see coming. There were crazy stories of all the usual types. Mostly it was a much better way to meet people and see places than reading in the big bookstores that tend to be very central. I was able to read in places that didn't even have bookstores and most of the people that attended weren't there for me, they were there because their friend was having a party. The majority of people at these parties had never been to a literary event in their life. It was really kind of amazing.

We all write for a reason, hopefully, our readers know that

that reason isn't money. **Why do you write?**

It's what I like to do. It fulfills me and connects me with others. I guess the question is almost, Why wouldn't I write? It's what I've been doing in my spare time for many years.

How does a book about writer's block and getting back onto adderall turn into a memoir, true-crime, substance-abuse, being a writer, and a love story, called The Adderall Diaries?

Well, it wasn't a book when I started. I just began taking notes, not worrying about writing a book or publishing, just kind of documenting my life and thoughts. I was trying to get out of my head, and about a week after I started that I heard that Sean Sturgeon confessed to 8-and-a-half murders (he wasn't sure if one of the victims was dead). Sean and I know a lot of people in common and our lives have overlapped in some very strange ways. So I started looking into that. But I still didn't know I was writing a book.

I've heard in a lot of interviews that you refer to your life as living like a retiree, do you still think that way? What's the best/worst part of that?

What I mean by that is I do what I want, I live the same life I would be living if I was retired and if I had a lot of money I don't think that would change too much. It's nice. I've learned to live on very little money and that's enabled me to not have a job. On the downside it would be impossible for me to support a family without going to work, and at this point going to work is out of the question.

With seven books under your belt, do you get recognized in San Francisco (or anywhere for that matter), when you're walking? How do you handle being known in that way?

Ha. I don't know. Occasionally at a party or something someone will recognize me, most likely because they saw me hosting a Rumpus event at The Makeout Room.

I noticed you have a few tattoos, what are they and what do they mean to you?

The one on the left arm is a cover up for a "jailhouse" tattoo I got in the group home when I was fourteen. It was huge, crooked dagger. The cover-up is a wizard releasing an orb. It's actually a western takeoff on a traditional eastern tattoo, but it's a greek figure instead of a buddha. On my left leg is The Persistence of Memory by Salvador Dali. I don't know why I did that one. I was in college and hanging out with the local tattoo artist and I said, Why don't you do that on my leg. The band on my right arm is actually a version of the leather pride flag. I got it early in my relationship with my ex-girlfriend, in 2005. I was in love, in that way that makes you literally crazy.

Your dad used to write bad reviews on Amazon.com about your books. What's the story behind this?

He still does stuff like that. It's mostly, I think, because he has a version of events that he doesn't think are being accurately represented in my books which frequently deal with my adolescence and time in group homes. Also, parents make a lot of sacrifices for their children, which I think he feels are overlooked in my writing and interviews.

You say in a lot of interviews that you stopped taking adderall and had writer's block. Why did you stop to begin with? Did you think it would have the effects it did?

I stopped taking Adderall because I wanted to be healthy and Adderall is amphetamine. I'd had writers block for a while before quitting Adderall.

You say on The Rumpus that you want to show people art and culture from people we haven't heard of, who are some of your favorite unknowns in the literary, art, and/or film, world?

I'm really fond of Ian Huebert, Paul Madonna, and Wendy MacNaughton in the art world. Though I don't know anything about art. Some writers that I think should receive more attention include Rob Roberge, Corrina Bain, Michelle Tea, and Bucky Sinister. But really, there's so many. A fair number of people have heard of Steve Almond and Rick Moody but they're both still under-appreciated.

If you could give one piece of advice to up and coming writers out there, that you wished you received when you started writing, what would it be?

You know, I wonder if such a thing exists. I don't know that I was really open to receiving advice when I was a young writer. I mean, I started writing when I was ten, and I was writing to get things off my chest, to express things that felt dangerous to say. Eventually I started publishing those things.

But you're really asking two separate questions. You're asking about advice for people who are starting to write and up and coming writers. If you're just starting to write you're probably ten years away from being an up and coming writer. If you're an up and coming writer I would say, keep the rights.

Are you working on anything new that you'd like to tell us about?

Just the Daily Rumpus emails.

How important is your education in regards to your writing?

I would say not very much. I never studied creative writing in college but when I was 29 I got a Stegner Fellowship to Stanford University. This was a big deal for me. It was validating and it gave me time to write. But in undergraduate I was a history major, then I did a one year master's degree in Cinema Studies.

How do you know when a book is "finished?"

That's a tough question. And it depends on the book. It's easier with a non-fiction present tense narrative like The Adderall Diaries, because you can literally run out of rope. A lot of finishing a novel for me is just not wanting to work on it anymore. I'm a compulsive re-writer. It takes a long time for that urge to drain from me.

What are your thoughts on basing your characters on real people?

I think it's OK. You should try to hide their identities if possible. If not possible you should write with fairness.

Thank you,
Goat

Bio

Stephen Elliott is the author of seven books including the memoir The Adderall Diaries and the novel Happy Baby. He is the founder of the online literary magazine The Rumpus. He recently finished directing his first feature film, Cherry.

Chad Kultgen

What comes to mind when you hear, "Mourning Goats?"

Sounds like a bad independent movie about some self-involved, depressed guy in his mid-twenties who inherits a goat farm from his dead estranged father. Something like the guy shows up at the farm to settle up with the bank, just sell the thing and be done with it, but then he runs into the wiser-than-her-years precocious girl who lives on the farm next door and he decides to stick around. While he's on the goat farm he learns valuable lessons about life and is forced to deal with the relationship he never had with his father and he comes to a new understanding of who his father was by performing the day to day activities that comprised his father's life on the goat farm for the last 15 years. In the end he doesn't fuck the girl, because he realizes she's far more than just a sexual encounter. She's his angel. She's the light that pulled him through the darkness of his life. There's a shitty soundtrack of overindulgent independent music. And I'd guess the family's last name is Goates.

You went to film school at USC, how did that affect your writing?

I'm not sure that it did all that much. USC taught me screenplay format. That was about it. Creatively I don't know that it had any impact on me. Certainly those four years in college were an important time to fuck around (with writing I mean) and figure out what I wanted to write about, what I thought was interesting or worth writing about, but in terms of teaching me technique or craft, I'd say USC had no impact. Watching and making movies to get a degree was fun, though. I highly recommend it if you don't care about your degree actually meaning anything to anyone once you graduate.

What can you tell us about your current project, Average American Marriage? Is it as delightfully honest as Average

American Male?

It's the same main character from the first book who is now married with little kids. I'd say it's at least as abrasive as the first book if not more so. There's something a little bit worse (at least to me) about the guy trying to masturbate with kids in the house or having sexual fantasies about pregnant women at baby showers.

What do you owe your success to? Selling over 100,000 of your first book is a phenomenon in today's market.

I don't know. I don't really think of myself as that successful. I guess when you throw that number out there it's technically successful, but until I have a New York Times bestseller or actually have enough money to buy a house in Los Angeles I'll just consider myself a guy who got lucky enough to be able to do what he loves for a living.

If someone wrote a book about me, even a negative book about me, I think I would take it as a complement, any experience with this?

I can only assume you're referring to the book my ex-girlfriend wrote that includes a section about our relationship, which she sold on the claim that one of my books (Average American Male) is about her (Hilary Winston – My Boyfriend Wrote A Book About Me). I don't take it as a compliment or an insult. She wrote a book about her life. I was a part of her life for a period of time and for a series of events that were significant to us both. She's a very smart and funny girl and I found those qualities reflected in what she wrote.

Your newest book is much different than your first two, do you think you'd like to write in a more literary way, or continue with the feeling of your first two books?

I've enjoyed the process of writing everything I've done – books, movies, tv shows. I don't have a set agenda on where I'd like to take my writing. I think the story and characters kind of inform the style of whatever I'm writing. So it's tough to say outright that I'd like to go in a more literary direction. My next book is a sequel to my first so at least for the time being, I'm going back to that style.

Do you feel like where you write directly affects what you write? What do you think LA does for your writing?

My writing location doesn't ever have any impact on the story, but it can certainly inform the details of the environment in which the story is told at least with the books I write. I'd say that I certainly like to know the places I'm setting a story in. I feel like the details of restaurants and movie theaters and malls and the various locations in a town make the story seem more real. So the Average American Male books were set in Los Angeles where I currently live. The Lie was Dallas, where I grew up. Men, Women and Children was Lincoln, Nebraska, which I've never even visited but did a lot of research about before writing the thing.

Do you really believe that if you're not moving to NYC, LA, or another large city, you're just waiting to settle down and make babies?

No. I don't think that at all. I don't know that actual statistics but I'd guess that people who move to larger cities to pursue some career in an industry that is rooted in one of those cities tend to start families later because they're initially focused on career. But that doesn't necessarily mean that if a person doesn't move to a big city, they're automatically only interested in "settling down and making babies."

In one interview, about your writing routine, you said, "It's very simple. If I'm not at the gym, playing video games, fucking, or drinking, I'm writing." That is the best routine I've ever heard! Do you find it easy to slip in to the mindset needed for each project or is it easy for you?

I'm glad you approve of my routine. I've always found it pretty easy to focus on whatever project I need to as deadlines dictate. The more different from one another they are the easier it is usually to switch from one to the other.

What's going on with Drones, your dark comedy being developed by FX?

I'm writing the pilot episode currently. I'll get some notes, do some rewrites and then see if I did a good enough job to actually get to make the pilot episode. Then if that turns out well, I'll see if I get a series order. Time will tell.

How do you think we're evolving with communication and information? Is instant access to everything helping the future or harming it?

I think it's definitely helping it. I don't see a scenario in which "instant access to everything" could harm the future. But no one's personal opinion on the rate of technological growth, good or bad, will change the fact that rapid expansion in communication technology will continue to happen.

As far as how I think we're evolving with communication and information – we're accepting it, embracing it and changing the way we live to make it a bigger part of our lives. When I was in high school the internet didn't really exist. Now the average high school kid not only has Facebook and Twitter, but they have a smart phone that gives them constant access to it. And these things (Facebook, Twitter, Smart Phones) are only interim technologies. They're only the first steps toward what seems like it will have to a kind of hive mind that we're all plugged into, a conduit that streams everyone's thoughts and feelings through everyone else's brains. It's like we're seeing the invention of the wheel but we also have the foresight to know that a car isn't far away.

You're currently in Texas for the holidays (I can only assume), is it a culture shock, going from LA to Texas?

I was in Texas for the holidays visiting my family. I don't know if it's a culture shock because I grew up in Texas so I know what to expect. But there are several differences between Texas and Los Angeles. The most apparent differences to me are that in Los Angeles every 3rd car is a Prius. In Texas every third car is an F150. Also there are many more Christian bumper stickers in Texas than in Los Angeles.

What's the deal with the squirrels?

If you're talking about the squirrels that live outside my kitchen window, the deal is that I feed them nuts.

Have you done any book tours or readings? How have they gone? Do you enjoy them?

I did a few for this last book. They were all bigger independent book stores in Portland, Denver, Los Angeles and New York. They were all great and I can't wait to go back to them with the Average American Male sequel next year. At a few of them I tested out a little performance art by making prank phone calls to the Trinity Broadcasting Network's prayer line and having them ask Jesus to make our next president a gay president. That's always fun.

You wrote an amazing article on mademan.com, Why Diamonds Are For...Suckers, do you write a lot of social commentary, like this? Where can we find some of it?

Thanks. I wish I did more, but that's really the only one I've done.

Do you think that writing has become much less lonely, nowadays? With Facebook, twitter, etc, it's easier to become a part of a community nowadays.

Was it lonely before? I don't know that I have anything to compare it to. I'm personally not lonely. I do like that the internet has made it much easier for people who read your stuff to contact you. I like hearing from people who have read my stuff, especially if they didn't like it. I know what I think of the stuff I write and it's always interesting to hear what someone else thinks of it.

In the interviews of yours that I've read, it says most of the writers you look up to are sci-fi writers, how do you explain the genre you write in compared to what you like to read?

Most of my favorite writers are all science fiction writers. I guess the stuff I do is pretty much the exact opposite of science fiction. It's as rooted in contemporary reality as I can make it. I don't know why that's the case. I guess the stuff I write doesn't necessarily entertain me. It interests me. Science fiction entertains me. It interests me, too, though. I really don't have a good answer for you on this one. Apologies.

Your writing feels like the kind of stream of conscious writing that goes through most people's minds, but is never said out loud. How did you go about selling your writing?

I'll assume you just want to know about the books and not the movies or TV shows. So the story of how I sold the books is as follows – I had agents for movies and TV and I had written a complete manuscript of The Average American Male that my feature and TV agents would sometimes send around as a writing sample. Eventually, I ended up selling The Average American Male to Showtime as a TV show. I wrote the pilot and they never made it. But through that process I was able to get a book agent who sold the book to Harper Perennial in under a month if I remember correctly (with the help of a young editor there who really championed the thing).

Harper was great to me. Everyone there really helped in getting the thing out there and it luckily did well enough that they wanted me to write some more books for them. That's the long and short of it.

I read your first two books on my kindle 3, what do you think of e-readers and what do you think they mean for literature?

I think they're great. I want as many people to be able to read my stuff as possible and it seems like the e-readers allow more people to be able to get access to it. As far as what they mean for the future of literature… that's a longer answer.

I don't really know what will happen to literature or to books in general, but every media industry (music was the first) is being forced to deal with this issue of no longer controlling the hard copy of their media. All media will eventually be delivered digitally and the hard copies will likely be produced in limited quantities for fans and collectors if that media format applies. Like video games, for example, I'll seriously doubt anyone will care if they own a hard copy of a video game in 5 years. But books and records I think will be around.

So it seems to me that model with books will most likely shift to something like 99% digital publishing and 1% of the market will be limited print run hardcovers, which will probably all be signed or come with some additional collectable packaging, of the huge titles that fans will buy.

I don't know that it will change the content of literature all that much, just the formatting. I think you'll start to see more and more, shorter novella type serialized series selling for 99 cents per "book." Things like that, but there will still be writers and there will still be people who want to read what they write.

What's next for Chad Kultgen, other than Average American Marriage?

I'm working on a bunch of different stuff – a few TV projects, a few movie projects, the book that will be after Average American Marriage, a comic book is floating into the mix. Basically I'm just writing as much as I can until people decide to stop letting me do it or I die.

What are your thoughts on basing your characters on real people?

I don't do it, although I have been accused of this by an ex girlfriend who then wrote an entire book about our relationship. That was fun.

What are the three biggest mistakes you made as a beginning writer?

The biggest one kind of encompasses all other smaller mistakes - not understanding how to make a living as a writer. Depending on what kind of things you're writing, there are different ways of going about getting paid for it. I graduated from film school and had no real idea how the industry of writing (books, TV, movies) worked in any capacity. In hindsight this information would have been far more valuable than any regarding the craft of writing. Initially there were a series of mistakes that involved sending my stuff to the wrong people or not sending the right material for a specific person to read or just generally having no idea how to even get my stuff read. I would lump all of these things into one larger mistake that I'll call being generally uninformed.

Do you have a favorite part about being a published writer?

My favorite part is probably just the fact being a writer has afforded me the ability to create a daily routine for myself that I wouldn't trade for anything. Wake up, go to the gym, eat lunch, write, get drunk, sleep, repeat. It's the best possible life I could have imagined for myself.

Thank you,

Goat

Bio

Chad was born in Spokane, WA. He grew up in Dallas, TX. He went to college in Los Angeles, CA where he currently resides. Chad writes books with high levels of sexually explicit content. He writes movies with far less sexually explicit content and TV shows with the least amount of sexually explicit content. He also play racquetball and feeds the squirrels that live outside his window. He's found that pecans are their favorite type of nut.

Chelsea Cain

What comes to mind when you hear, "Mourning Goats?"

Sad goats. Specifically, the goat I had as a kid. Her name was
Full Moon and I was weaned on her milk. I loved that goat. She
got old and sick and my mother wanted to put her out of her
misery, so she hired someone to do it. He came by when we
weren't home and shot Full Moon in the head with a shotgun. We
came home and she was just lying there dead in her pen. My
mother felt terrible about that. Big guilt. I don't remember it. I'm
not sure if I didn't see her, or if I just blocked it out. I was in my
early twenties by the time my mom finally told me the story. She
still felt terrible, after all those years. They buried her in the yard
at that house. I went by there about a year ago and they had torn
down the old farmhouse and built a mcmansion. But somewhere
underneath it all are the bones of my old goat.

**Fellow Mourning Goats interviewee, Monica Drake, is in a
writing workshop with you and Chuck Palahniuk, what are
your thoughts on this? Do you think being in a group like this
has been a big part of your success?**

It certainly helped me with the first book – Heartsick. When I
joined the group, I was about 180 pages into Heartsick and I
spent a year bringing it in a chapter at a time and rewriting it. I
knew nothing about how to write fiction. And that group was like
taking a master class. They are all so incredibly smart about
writing, and gifted at different aspects of the craft. Of course we
are also all nuts, so I think it's good that we all have somewhere
we can go once a week to remind ourselves that we are not alone,
and to keep us off the streets so we don't hurt ourselves. I've been
in writing groups before and personally I find them really useful.
But it depends on you, and it depends on who's in your group.
Find people who make a living writing. Ideally people who have
MFAs, and know stuff. People who are serious about it. And meet

on neutral ground. Don't meet at someone's house. Meet at an office. Find a room at a library. Meet every week. And if it's the wrong group, disband and find another one. Eventually, you will find your people.

What was it like going to number 8 on the New York Times bestseller list with Heartsick? As great as it must have been, was it stressful in any way?

That was up there with the birth of my daughter as a Best Life Moment. Okay, it was better than the birth of my daughter. That is probably a terrible thing to say – but it's totally true. I was in San Francisco, and my publisher and editor called me from a bar in New York where they were already celebrating. There was lots of shouting. I wanted to go right out and get a tattoo. One, to commemorate the event, and two, because I figured that for the rest of my life people would ask me what I had the number 8 tattooed on my bicep, and that would be an excuse to tell them that I was a NEW YORK TIMES BEST SELLING AUTHOR, THANKS FOR ASKING. That night I did a reading in S.F., and no one came. Not a single person! Maybe if I'd gone through with the tattoo...

I saw you were thinking about giving out personalized floaty pens on your next book tour, have you done anything like this in the past? How did it go?

I've given out all sorts of stuff. "I 'heart' Archie/Gretchen" buttons. Severed fingers. Severed hands and feet. Rhinestone heart pins. Jelly-filled people-shaped donuts with pretzel stabbed in them. Temporary tattoos. I'm always looking for novelty items to give away. I guess I'm trying to make my readings an event. A show. On my last tour, I got friends to write murder ballads about Gretchen and perform them at a few of my readings. There are so many authors and so many readings and so many bookstores, it just feels like anything extra helps. If I could tap dance, I would.

How does one write humor for The Oregonian, reviews for

New York Times, and horror that leaves the reader in physical pain?

Horror and farce aren't so different in terms of structure. It's all about tension and reveal, timing, and the unexpected. People are always so surprised to discover that I'm funny. But I think my thrillers are funny. Dark. But funny. And I think it's important in a tense and nail-biting narrative to give the reader a break. Maybe not a belly laugh—but the occasional wry smile. Or at least a fleeting smirk.

I love the story on your website about wanting to be a firedog as a little girl, I think we all had big dreams as children, were your parents very supportive of the firedog? Being a writer?

My parents told me that I could be anything I wanted. And I swear to you, I really believed that I could be a fire dog. I was four or five by the time I realized that it was pretty much an impossibility to will oneself into becoming a Dalmatian. I guess my parents didn't want to limit my potential. The only pressure I felt about what to do when I grew up was that I should choose something that would make me happy. My mother thought I should be a stand-up comedian. (I don't know where she got this – because I was not a funny kid at all). The only time my dad ever seemed disappointed in me professionally was when I called him up at a low point and told him I wanted to go to law school. By the time we got off the phone he had talked me out of it.

I read about the tattoo on your right shoulder, can you tell the readers what it is and what it means?

I have two tattoos. I think you're talking about the one on my left bicep. It's a tattoo of a snake. Snakes are my one irrational fear, and I thought that by tattooing one on my arm, I could claim the fear and conquer it. It didn't work, but it's a nice tattoo.

Which is scarier and why? The worlds that you come up with in your writing, or dropping your little girl off at kindergarten for the first time?

Oh, God – Kindergarten. A friend once told me that dropping your kid off for the first day of kindergarten was like throwing a puppy out the window of a moving car onto the highway. I think that's a pretty apt description.

The advanced readers copy of Heartsick is beautiful, it's a white cover with a bloody hand smudge grabbing the book, what happened to that cover? Did you love it? Maybe this can be transferred to the movie poster?

Thanks! That is a great galley. They thought it was too gory for the general public. But there's a Japanese edition of Heartsick that used the design. It's tiny and square and completely cute in that particular Japanese way, and yet also blood spattered and disturbed. Naturally, I love it.

I read in an interview that you were planning on continuing to write humor books, under a pseudonym, can you give us any info on this? Are you working on anything?

I'd like to do one in the future at some point. I miss those books. I loved the collaboration with the illustrator. Writing is such a solitary gig. There's interaction. You work with an agent, an editor, marketing people, and then when it's out in the world, there are readers and media people. But mostly it's you pulling threads of ideas out your nose and trying to knit something out of them. I love working with an illustrator throughout the creative process. We inspire one another. There's an energy to that that is absolutely thrilling. As soon as I think of an idea— and find three months of free time—I'll get right on that.

You wrote your first book, Dharma Girl, and got it published in your early twenties, what do you feel has changed the most in your writing since then?

My advance for Dharma Girl was $1000. My advances now have a lot more zeros. It's just completely different. My whole approach is different. I am part of something much larger, and there is more pressure, and I feel more responsibility. This is my career, not a side project. I wrote Dharma Girl by instinct. It's all gut. I am much more purposeful and thoughtful about my writing now. I guess that comes with practice. Along with bad eyesight and cynicism.

Again, with Dharma Girl, you say on your website that it is your favorite, why?

Dharma Girl is the story of my return to the hippie commune where I spent my early childhood. It is the book that was burning to get out. It's youthful and intuitive and reckless and raw, but it will always be my favorite. It's the book I had in me – the story I had to tell. And it's such a valentine to my parents and to my early childhood and to my mom (who died a few months before it was published). It's not my best book. But it has a huge place in my heart.

I don't like how everyone focuses around you being a woman (men and women can be equally sick in my mind), what are your thoughts on this kind of attention?

It baffles me. Just last week a woman approached me at an event and asked me, "How can you write these books, as a woman?" She was smiling, just making conversation. But I was completely blind-sided. It's like asking someone how he can be a doctor as a redhead. It doesn't compute to me. I think of myself as a thriller writer, not a female thriller writer.

For all of our aspiring authors out there, what advice would you give them on writing? What do you wish someone told you when you started out in this career?

My most sage advice is the trickiest: you will never make a living writing, until you learn to write when you don't want to.

Thank you for giving your readers permission to laugh at your books! I think some of the subject matter is so scary and disgusting that laughter is the only thing that makes it okay. What's one of the sickest or most disgusting things you've written that you laughed at?

I've always thought that pulling someone's small intestine out with a crochet hook was pretty funny.

Which was more of an influence in starting this series, the Green River Killer or the hormones of pregnancy? I've read you comment on both in other interviews.

I couldn't have written Heartsick without the influence of both.

What have your tours been like? Are there a lot of interesting fans? Any scary stories?

I'm sort of disappointed at the normalcy and sweetness of my fans. I expected more mouth breathers carrying axes. But the vast majority of my readers are quite upstanding. I do get the occasional creepy email or letter from people who like my books for, shall we say, the wrong reasons.

I read an interview from the early 2000's and it seems like you never saw these books coming, was writing this series out of left field for you? A happy accident?

That first book was out of left field. I'd always loved reading thrillers and watching cop shows on TV. I had that idea for the first book, and halfway through writing it, I came up with the idea of writing a series because I had so many ideas for the characters and didn't want to cram everything into one novel. But I had no idea how huge they would be. I still pinch myself. I am covered with bruises from all the pinching.

What's next for Chelsea Cain? Can you tell us anything about your next project?

The Night Season (book four in the series) comes out March 1, 2011, and I'm working on book five. Gretchen moves off stage for most of The Night Season, so Archie and Susan and Henry have some room to grow as characters. There's a new serial killer on the loose, and Portland is threatened by massive flooding. There is so much water in this book that I had to start looking up synonyms. I ran out of ways to describe wet. It's a good old-fashioned heart-stopper of a thriller. Less gore, and more action. Lots of fun to write. It's also a good entry point to the series. I wanted to write a book that people could read without having to read all the other books leading up to it. But that would still be satisfying to loyal readers of the series. Is that convincing enough? Have you ordered a copy? Please order a copy. I'll tap dance...

Heartsick, Sweetheart, and Evil at Heart are your last three novels, are you going to miss heart in the title of your new book, due in March 2011, The Night Season?

Not at all. I have a list of hundreds of heart titles they are each sillier than the last. I'm excited to have some freedom. Talk to me in a few books. I'll be back to "Heartburn."

How important is your education in regards to your writing?

What a great question. College gives you time to write. I didn't get an MFA, but I got a masters in journalism, and I used that time to write my first book, Dharma Girl. College may seem like it takes a lot of time, what with those occasional classes and all that hanging out in bars, but it takes a lot less time that a full time job, believe me. Also, writing programs offer something way more useful than poetry readings and massive debt – they offer contacts. My first book found a publisher because a professor took an interest and helped connect me to an editor. So I guess I fall in the education camp. That can be college, it can be workshops or retreats, it can be sitting around bullshitting with people smarter than you are. I still meet with a weekly writing group and those people have taught me everything I know about how to write fiction. I've published four NY Times bestsellers, and I still read books on how to write a goddamn novel. I'm still flying by the seat of my pants. Any chance I have to listen to a writer lecture, or read a craft article, I take it.

How do you know when a book is "finished?"

Never. Ever. You just give up. Or reach a point where it is "good enough." I mean, the thing has to get published at some point. I think that most new writers think they're finished too soon, when what they have is a complete first draft. It's not enough for you to think that your book is good enough; other people have to think so, too. A good rule of thumb is, once you have a complete first draft and think you're done, spend a year going through it page by page making it better. Then start asking yourself and other people if it's done. For what it's worth, I keep editing even after a book is published. My reading copies are always scribbled out with stuff written in the margins. I re-write every paragraph as I'm reading at a bookstore. I can always find stuff to like when I go back and look at past books, but I can always find stuff that makes me want to spoon out my eyes, too.

What are your thoughts on basing your characters on real people?

I think it's a bad idea. This caught me up for a long time. I'd base a character on someone I knew and then start second guessing the character. Betsy wouldn't really say that. I only started writing passable fiction when I gave myself permission to make up characters out of whole cloth. That way I could control them without Betsy looking over my shoulder. And believe me, Betsy can be a real pain in the ass.

Thank you,
Goat

Bio

Chelsea Cain is the author of The New York Times bestselling thrillers HEARTSICK, SWEETHEART, EVIL AT HEART, and THE NIGHT SEASON. KILL YOU TWICE comes out in August 2012. Her Portland-based thrillers, described by The New York Times as "steamy and perverse," have been published in over 30 languages, recommended on "The Today Show," appeared in episodes of HBO's "True Blood" and ABC's "Castle," named among Stephen King's top ten favorite books of the year, and included in NPR's list of the top 100 thrillers ever written. According to Booklist, "Popular entertainment just doesn't get much better than this."

Rick Moody

What comes to mind when you hear, "Mourning Goats?"

The French collage technique known as the faux raccord, in which two apparently disparate and disjunctive elements are yoked together, according to the promptings of the unconscious, if by no other agency, in order to see what energy might result.

You've been doing a lot of interviews for your newest book, The Four Fingers of Death, what questions are you sick of answering?

Actually, I did a lot of interviews last year. I haven't done any in four or five months, and this is a blessing. This pause. And yet as some time has passed any question seems new today, including this one. I'm more sick of questions about the film called The Ice Storm, and the film called Garden State, which had nothing to do with me, than I am sick of questions about Four Fingers, which in spite of everything still seems like a dark horse of a book, and one, at least for the moment, that I still kind of like. So questions along those lines are gratefully received.

Rick Moody, life coach? Can you tell us a little bit about what your thought process behind literature saving lives is?

I personally treat literature as though it is deadly serious — even when it's very funny (and I like comic-flavored stuff a lot) — as though it were more important than other things. Way more important than television, e.g., way more important than Lady Gaga, or even Animal Collective, way more important than whatever indie film is hot at the moment. And I want other people to feel the same way. It's almost inexplicable to me that other people don't agree already. "Rick Moody, Life Coach," which began as a shaggy dog story, for my web site, has lately become deadly serious, and I am somewhat pleased that it has done so. Feel free to ask an advice question there, if it suits you: www.hatredofnaturalism.com.

You've taught at a few schools, are you teaching now and do you believe that creativity can be taught?

I don't believe that "creativity" can be taught, but I believe that "bad prose" can be corrected with a few handy tricks. I also think that neurosis can be circumnavigated, so as to make literary writing less narcissistic. This is easy to encourage, and when I have done so, when I have encouraged, I often find that there are much improved results among the student body. Whether they are "creative" or not. And who cares about "creative," really? It's sort of romanticist crap. Everything is creative. Painting surfboards, designing automobiles, drizzling that maroon gunk around the base of your piece of cheesecake.

Yes, this week I am teaching at NYU.

In addition to writing fiction, you're also a composer and musician, do you believe that writing music and writing fiction go hand in hand, or are they two different worlds?

I'm not actually a composer, because that would involve staves and clefs and dotted quarter notes, and so on. I am not a very able reader of scores. I am, however, a songwriter, which can be done mostly by ear, at least at my level. I am a lyricist, and sometimes I am a writer of melodies and harmonies too. I am a singer of some minimal ability. And a very bad player of guitar and piano. I don't, in the end, feel that music and literature are so very different, because they are both auditory phenomena. Language, that is, has a musical aspect, even when it is on a page. You hear the music in your internal register of sounds. And I think, therefore, that playing music makes me a better writer. And: it's less lonely than writing words down on a page, at least if you do it in a band context.

When you started writing, you decided you were going to be a short story writer, what pushed you to start writing novels?

There were two reasons: 1) novels were easier to sell, and I wanted to be published, somehow, if only to see what that experience was like, and 2) I felt as though I would never be legit-imate if I didn't try to do it—make a novel—at least once. This was my own neurotic rationale, but there it is. Somehow I got away with publishing a very primitive novel. So I kept going.

Who's your first reader and why?

It changes with each project. I don't feel it's right to burden a person more than once with this onerous task. Because the person has to be willing to tell me the truth, and I sometimes make it relatively uncomfortable for them. I cause trouble when I don't like the truth, at least at first.

Where do you see language going? Is technology hindering or helping?

Technology is both hindering and helping. I find, in general, that digital culture is a force for ill. I don't think the Kindle or the iPad are so tremendous. I think they dumb things down a bit. (And a reasonable proximation of this effect is seen in the indefensible tendency of the Apple Corporation to capitalize the names of their devices like idiots.) And I think these e-readers are going to change publishing monetarily in a way that makes it less good for writers, makes it harder to stay alive and write, and that is bad for serious fiction, because serious fiction is the first thing to go when publishers are afraid about money. To put it another way: straight-to-Kindle is a great publishing idea if you write vampire books.

That said, e-mail, generally speaking, was a development that I welcomed with open arms, because it made it possible for me to ignore my telephone more. Which is a blessing. I delight in typing answers to questions rather than speaking them. I think I do a better job when I am in text mode. Whether text mode will last, however, is another question. When impatient types can use a video interface to the exclusion of the written word, then we are back to an infantile linguistic culture again.

You're a voracious reader, what's on your night stand now?

I'm judging a prize right now so I'm reading a lot of very

popular stuff that I missed before. I shouldn't name names, but it's all very popular. Also: Samson Agonistes by John Milton.

Which is your favorite form to write in, fiction, non-fiction, short stories? Why?

No favorite. Each form energizes the others.

In an interview from 2009, you said that after your baby was born you felt like you changed a little, and that you would be "more direct, less inclined to waste time," do you see that coming out in your newer work?

I'm wasting more time, actually! And I watch it get wasted with a grim feeling about the whole thing. But it's true that I'm trying to be a bit more serious than in the last three books. And there's more about parenting, and about sympathy for parents, in this new manuscript. So far. But who knows. I'm only six months into this project.

Compared to the other Mourning Goats interviewees, I noticed that there are a lot of youtube videos of you, is this something you've purposely done for marketing, or it just happens that you enjoy being videoed?

Actually, being videotaped makes me want to curl up into a ball and die. I had nothing to do with most of those recordings, although I try to accept that this is part of life. Shut up and do your job and quit complaining, etc. I never watch video documentation of myself. Excepting the one where I threw the pie at Dale Peck. I watched that one once. The ones where I speak make me want to die. My voice and my person and the inter-facing of the two: horrifying, really. I can't imagine being the kind of person who thinks this is a good thing, believe me. Maybe Anderson Cooper thinks it is a good thing? No, I bet he never watches the stuff either.

You have a music blog on therumpus.net, how did this come about, and why do you do it?

Stephen Elliott asked. I probably wouldn't have done it for anyone else. But I believe in Stephen's crazy ambition and his hydra-headed empire, and so I thought I'd give it a shot. Initially, I imagined I was going to write a paragraph once a week, without revising, but what happened was that I started to care, and so now the installments are these twenty-page essays that require an enormous amount of work and forethought. So I'm doing it much less frequently than I originally thought. But I am still relatively pleased with the results. There's a new piece up there right now. About John Lurie.

In a lot of interviews you say that location is important for writing. How do you think it affects what you write and how you write? Is it the surroundings, the people, the distractions, or what?

I think setting is a character in the work, if that's not oxymoronic, or excessively paradoxical. At least it's so in the books I like. Think of Dublin in ULYSSES, or the sea in Conrad or Melville. Or the Alps in THE MAGIC MOUNTAIN. Those books are unthinkable deprived of their settings. I guess now I am interested in settings that are not northeastern suburbs or urban settings. I am tired of books about places I have lived. So I try to go in search of new places, in the hopes that these places will inspire me a bit. Some places are useless. New Jersey is useless to me now. So is Omaha, Nebraska. But the desert! Now that is a place that could inspire you! My sad lot is that now I have to try to get the same feeling out of Springfield, Missouri. For the new book.

When you write, you sometimes have multiple projects open at the same time on your computer, it's impressive that you can focus on each individually, how do you think this affects the way you write? Do you feel like the stories influence each other as you're writing?

Life is lived this way now, with multiple projects always going. Many people, many writers, are like this now, except for people who are more impressively Luddite than I am. I like Luddism. It appeals. But I sort of don't have as much time for it as I'd like. I have no land line in my writing studio now, and no television, and even no Internet in the actual writing space. But there are other ways that the historical moment creeps in. I'm trying to answer this entire question without using the word "m— —t— — —." As I am also trying to suggest that the fragmentary qualities of the present are the present in some ways, and that is okay. And, yes, things influence each other a little bit. One set of fragments influences another set.

You received your MFA from Columbia University, were you happy with the program, and would you do it again if given the opportunity?

Nope.

Your newest novel, The Four Fingers of Death, is over 700 pages, how hard is it to keep something that long, straight in your head? Is this your longest work (published or not)?

It's the longest. But THE DIVINERS was threatening to be rather long. It's not so hard to keep long things in your head. You just have to believe in the project, you know? And then whatever emerges from you is part of the project. After the fact you can organize it into something coherent. I believe in absolute liberation in draft one, and absolute dictatorship in draft two.

Do you have a set writing schedule or do you write when the urge hits? What advice do you have for the writers out there reading this blog? What's next for Rick Moody?

These three questions are all pretty standard, and since you asked above about questions that I get asked most frequently, let me say that each of these is on the list. So maybe you won't mind if I try to randomize these questions and see if there is a hidden agenda! An allusion to the illuminati or something. Here's a question, that is, in fact, made out of every third word of your trifecta:

Have writing do when hits do for out this next moody?

A: Exactly. I never know when it's going to strike, but sometimes when the interstellar strains of radio noise are such as to control the hypnagogic voices, I no longer have a need to kill kill kill, and I am able to see the future and what it beholds. Cephalopods. Arachnids. Flesh-eating bacteria. Medieval religious cults. Cyborgs. Trepanning.

How do you know when a book is "finished?"

When I have changed "which" to "that," a few times.

What are three mistakes you made as a beginning writer?

Lack of absolute faith in my vision. Believing that I had to be a little more "accessible" in order to be published. Worrying, ever, about a readership.

Do you have a favorite part about being a published writer?

People send me things.

Thanks,

Goat

Bio

Rick Moody is the author of five novels, three collections of stories, a memoir, and, most recently, a collection of essays, ON CELESTIAL MUSIC. He also plays in and writes songs for The Wingdale Community Singers.

Joey Goebel

What comes to mind when you hear, "Mourning Goats?"

I picture some gnarly young billy goats at a funeral home—
Dave Coulier types. You know, sophisticated and petite, but with
a little extra torque in the squat-thrusting department. One of
them arrives and signs in at the guest book on the little podium
with the pull-string lamp and thinks, "It never fails—no one
signs their address in these things. They only sign their name,
even though it clearly asks for the name and address. Screw it,
I'm signing my name and address. That's what it asks for, so why
shouldn't I?" So then this goat walks inside and licks some asses
and gets his ass licked, and he goes over to one of the sitting
areas where the family has set up a computer slideshow of the
recently deceased goat as a child, with his family, dressed as
Brian Austin Green for Halloween, etcetera, etcetera, what will
be will be. But then Lyle starts thinking, "Ah, man. That might
make me look self-important—like I think I'm special in some
old-fashioned way—the way I decided to be the first one to put
my address, while so many others just signed their names." So
he goes back and eats the entire guest book and leaves.

**One of my favorite stories of yours is The Phallic Artist,
from a now defunct journal, Cellar Door, did you write that
during the same time you wrote Torture the Artist? I felt like
they were connected in a lot of ways.**

I wrote it not long after I finished Torture the Artist, and
you're right; the theme of The Phallic Artist is identical to that of
Torture. The story behind that is that someone at the publishing
house asked me to write a companion piece to Torture the Artist,
such as a short story that could be placed somewhere in order to
spread the word about the book. I got the idea from a friend who
was in a figure drawing class in college. He would call me up
almost every night and share with me his acute anxiety over

having to draw a nude male model. He was seriously considering leaving the drawing blank at the crotch area. To comfort him, I said, "Who knows—maybe because you're so worried about this, your heightened emotions will come through when you draw dicks, and maybe you'll be so good at drawing them that you will have found your calling." I could see him screaming to the heavens: "Damn this gift I've been given!" He ended up getting through it without any trauma, and I got a story out of it. I don't know what happened with getting it published, but a couple of years later I eventually placed the storymyself when Cellar Door asked for a piece. It was then made into a short film by Lucky Rabbit Films out of Austin.

I saw that Pat Walsh was your editor for The Anomalies, what can you say about him? Also, editors in general, what have they done for you?

Pat is very intelligent and has a great sense of humor. Not only is he intelligent in terms of the writing side of publishing, but also the business side of publishing. There was a long stretch of time—I guess from The Anomalies on through Torture the Artist—that I talked to him far more than I talked to any of my closest friends. I loved talking to him. He was good at making me feel good—which I think is a good trait for an editor. We had a lot of laughs. I remember the one time he did not laugh is when I made fun of California for electing Arnold Schwarzenegger as governor. (I had to say something as it was nice to see another state embarrassing itself.) He took that one hard. He didn't see any humor in that. What have editors done for me? Well, in Pat's case, he got my novel-writing career started by reading my query letter and then asking for my manuscript. In general, I think editors are helpful for the author's morale. The relationship with editors isn't exactly what I'd thought it be; there haven't been any in-depth series of letters about the writing itself, like with F. Scott Fitzgerald and Maxwell Perkins. Usually with editors, I talk more about business than the books themselves. I always enjoy talking to them.

I love the line you wrote, "Get mad at something and make it better through writing." What did you get mad about for each of your books?

For The Anomalies, I got mad at how predictable everyone was. With so many people, you know what they're all about without them even opening their mouth. Their appearance is their mold and everything about them fits into that mold. And as a result, so many people are basically the same, because they so often "look the part" and vice versa. ("Haven't we met before?" I would find myself thinking.) For Torture the Artist, I got mad at how utterly stupid and talentless the entertainers of the 21st century had become. I was—and still am—gobsmacked at what passes for entertainment. And for Commonwealth, I got mad that American voters not once but twice elected a man into office who did not represent their economic interests. All the contradictions stared us in the face: a common man who was a member of one of the most elite families in the country, the more masculine choice who was also a cheerleader. All I can do is barf, and the barf comes out in book form. "Goebel" is slang for vomit in German, which I've been made aware of repeatedly when I tour over there.

Do you write every day? Every week? What does the writing process look like, for you?

I do write every week, normally Monday through Friday.

I'm still trying to find the best process. Sometimes I do it according to time: As long as I put in approximately seven to eight hours a day into my book (as well as in book-related tasks, like answering e-mails or going through my notes), then I'll be satisfied. Or lately, I've been doing it by quota: six pages a day. This is in an attempt to get the first draft done for my new novel. It's a triumph psychologically to finish the first draft, which I find to be the most difficult.

In Torture the Artist, you described something beautiful

and horrible rolled into one, what do you think about where entertainment is going these days? Should we start some experiments, see what we can create?

Entertainment is as ghastly as ever. It's gotten worse since I wrote Torture the Artist. My views on this topic can best be expressed in a song I wrote for my new recording project (which I'm calling Nervous People). The song is called "Bodies Writhing (the American Music Awards)": Bodies on the TV, dancin' up a stormCallin' themselves artists, I'm callin' it pornI can hear the message, rubbin' it's way through: You were awful slutty, now I'll have to outslut you

Yes, sweeheart I see you, yes, you're all grown up. Maybe someday we'll forget your Mickey Mouse Club. Yes, I said I see you, you're bringin' sexy back. Substituting lust for the talent that you lack. Chorus—Looks like they've made love obsolete. Where once there was warmth, there's only heat And bodies writhing. This is what it's come to: Ga Ga Boom Boom PowBaby caveman orgies make that future sound. No imagination, but man, they sure can move. Looks like they're thinking anything but thinking ought to do

Repeat chorus. Bridge: Touch my body, won't you touch my body? Repeat chorus and bathe. I don't think any experiments would succeed. The best we can hope for is that the occasional work of true originality and imagination will reach mainstream audiences. LOST would be an example. I am a full-blown LOST fanatic. From a writing standpoint, I've never seen a show that's so ambitious. And the different narrative techniques they used throughout the six seasons always impressed me.

You were awarded Romania's Ovid Festival Prize in 2009. How did an author from Kentucky win this? What did it entail?

My novels were published in Romanian, and the judges noticed, I guess. And the reason I was published in Romanian is because I was published in German by Diogenes, the largest independent publisher in Europe. They are well-connected all over the globe, and they handle my foreign rights, so that's how I ended up getting published in all the various countries. To receive the award, I got a trip to Romania, and I brought my wife with me. We were right on the Black Sea in a town called Neptun that was formerly a resort for the communist higher-ups. I attended some conferences and went to readings, and it culminated with the awards ceremony. I tore it up, author-style. The whole trip was surreal for me, and the prize money allowed me to focus solely on writing and doing water colors of ear lobes for several months.

With that, it seems that you have a huge following in Europe, do you think America will catch up?

Well, check this out: ELLE Magazine in Romania made my book one of their book club picks, and so I did an event in Bucharest, Romania, where all these young Romanian ladies were gathered to discuss my book. My wife and I got a kick out of that, especially since it took place in a high-end furniture store. I've never read ELLE, but I would imagine the American version of ELLE doesn't offer much page-time for authors or books. Who would want to read about books when we can read about which cast member of CSI: New York Angeles has the best set of abdominal muscles or learn about how great Kate Hudson's fallopian tubes are? So from what I've observed, authors aren't as marginalized by the media in Europe. Let me put it this way: If America "catches up" as you put it, I'd be surprised, unless I come up with some good plots for lonely vampire wolves.

You've been doing some freelance work this past year, how did it go? Anything you're particularly proud of?

It went well. It's sad how much more money I could make writing an article about Michael Jackson than I could being an educator. I liked the Michael Jackson piece because it made me feel like I was a part of this big news story, rather than just an observer. DIE ZEIT contacted me, like, the Thursday after he died, and I had to have it turned in by Monday. They wanted a younger American's take on what he meant to pop culture. I discovered that with my ability to get published in the German papers and magazines, freelance work is relatively easy money, but what I don't like about it is that it took away from my creative writing time.

You did your MFA in a low-residency program, after you'd already been published, what did you think of the program, and why go back after tasting success?

I went back after being published because I wanted the security of having a master's degree so that I could get a "real" job. When it comes to my books, I never know from one year to the next how much money I'm going to make, so getting an MFA was something I decided to do when I knew that I would be getting married and eventually reproducing. So basically, it was the decision of rational guy being uncertain of his financial future. Oh—and I wanted to enrich myself intellectually. I was more than pleased with the program. I chose Spalding University, which is in Louisville. The workload was daunting, but I thrived under all the deadlines, and these deadlines helped me write Commonwealth, probably the longest book I'll ever write. It was actually such a positive experience that I found it disconcerting. I kept thinking, "Why is this going so well?" The teachers were wise and my classmates were supportive. Some people say that the problem with these MFA programs is that they churn out batches of writers who all write the same way, and that they are therefore institutions breeding conformity. But you hear that argument so often that I think it's just become something that people think they are supposed to say, kind of like when people say that Kanye West is a musical genius.

I read on a German site, that you're teaching now, what books are you using with your students? Any of your own?

I teach English 101 and 102, so they mostly have to read textbooks. However, I make it a point to have them read one novel, and one of their essays is supposed to be about that novel. I make them a list of novels that are either classics or ones that I think they'd like. I also usually pick short ones, for obvious reasons. One semester, I assigned only five novels, so that we could have five in-depth discussions about some of my favorite novels. These novels were: Cat's Cradle, The Metamorphosis, The Great Gatsby, The Catcher in the Rye, and The Stranger. It amazes me when someone doesn't like any one of these books.

What's happening with the Torture the Artist movie, with Lucky Rabbit Films?

I don't have much to report. The producers have optioned the film rights a third time, and they are very much interested in making the film a reality. They flew to Kentucky to meet me and my wife. I liked them, and I patiently await to see what they do with the book.

Last year you wrote, "The song is so bad that while I was listening to it, it made me dislike life," in reference to an Owl City song, topping the charts. I laughed out loud, or lol'd as the kids are saying, when I read that, any new songs you particularly hate or would like to rip apart?

I LOVE this question. I had forgotten that line, which I used on ye ol' Facebook, I believe. Since you've brought it to my attention, I think I'll make a place for it in my new novel, so thanks. There are so many new songs that I hate, and you might think, "Why do you listen to them, then?" But I think it's good to be aware of them. It's kind of like checking the pulse of youth culture, to see how much longer it will be before the world dies off. So every once in a while, in the car, I'll listen to the pop stations, and I also watch the big music award shows, and I'll sit there in a state of pure wonder, saying to myself, "This is REAL. This is not a Saturday Night Live skit. This is not meant to be a joke. And people LIKE it." A perfect example would be the Black Eyed Peas updated version of "I Had the Time of My Life." Okay, that in itself is stupid enough (Can't you hear them pitching it to the record execs—"Yo, we wanna take that Dirty Dancing song and make it our own.") But then—after Will I Am and Fergie struggle out the chorus, they inexplicably start saying "dirty bit" as the song falls apart into a techno atrocity. It is SO BAD. And then—this was at the aforementioned American Music Awards— when it was over, Will I Am yelled, "Welcome to the future." So here is the future, everyone: the song from Dirty Dancing and the repetition of the words "dirty bit"...the complete absence of creativity or originality...And have you seen how they dress? My twelve-month-old niece has a cooler fashion sense than the Black Eyed Peas. They look like idiots. A couple of more observations from the American Music Awards: When certain buxom chanteuses like Katy Perry and Rihanna came out wearing dresses that actually covered themselves, I announced to my wife, "That dress is coming off within thirty seconds." And I was right... You know those background dancers who basically just straddle things and writhe on the floor? I always think about how they have parents: "Hey, Mom! Be sure to watch me on the American Music Awards tonight. I'll be dryhumping Ne-Yo's thigh. Be sure to tell all your friends." Why the hell hasn't Justin Bieber's voice changed yet? Isn't he going on 18 by now? Does he have some sort of developmental problem? Is he a castrato? Sidenote: My sister always comments about how Justin Bieber gives her the creeps, which I think is hilarious, and I kind of see what she means. And two more songs that I'd like to address: Bruno Mars has a hit song called "Just the Way You Are." Why?! You know that he or someone in his camp HAD to know the title was already taken by Billy Joel. I think it was an arrogant choice to call the song that. I mean, how did it even happen? Was he listening to the radio and heard the BillyJoel song and say, "Hmm. Since I can't come up with an original idea, I'll just take that chorus word-for-word but change everything else about the song." Bruno's song is melodramatic, with a melody that I would call "obvious," and "easy" lyrics. There isn't a tenth of the melodic appeal of the Billy Joel song. (And don't get me started on how Billy Joel is always considered "uncool.") And Ke$ha has a lyric in her song that says "we're dancing like we're dumb." Finally, a 21st century performer who sings the truth.

When you wrote Torture the Artist, you said that you had a much darker ending in mind, before meeting your wife, where did you originally see it going?

I think I was going to have the Harlan character just wither away in his hotel room. Strangely, even with the way I ended up writing it, I've had a lot of readers and interviewers comment on what a sad, bleak ending it is. But it's supposed to be happy.

You wrote four screenplays earlier in your career, do you ever think about turning any of the three left into novels (The Anomalies was a screenplay before being published as a novel)?

No, because they're low-brow comedies, and anyone who still reads novels in the 21st century would not be interested in reading stupid comedies. Here were the titles: FRANKY DANDELION, THE SCHOOL OF WHATNOT, and GIRL HUNT. I've written several more since I became a novelist, and I plan to continue writing them. For me, screenplays are much, much easier than novels.

When you send out books to fans, I've seen on more than one occasion that you send out old pictures of teen idols, what's the story behind this and do you still do it? (I personally got Bruce Springsteen and Rob Lowe)

Ha! You fared better than most. Just yesterday I sent out C. Thomas Howell and Rachel Ward. My sister was a teenager in the 1980's, and she would buy the Teen Bop magazines, and I'm assuming they still have magazines like this—each page would simply be a photo of a teen idol, everyone from the cast of the Breakfast Club to Andrew McCarthy to El Debarge to Scott Valentine. My sister would cut her favorites out and cover an entire bedroom wall with them, and because I wanted to be just like my big sister, I did the same thing, even though it was probably inappropriate for a six-year-old boy to have his walls plastered with pictures of Judd Nelson and Patrick Duffy. (I also really liked female soap opera stars of the '80s and had an album full of pictures of Emma Samms and Finola Hughes and Felicia from General Hospital. I was a weird little dude, even back then.) So my sister saved these old magazines. What people get in the mail from me are the pictures of celebrities that my sister and I didn't deem wall-worthy. Yes, I still do it, though my supply is nearly depleted. I do it just because I like the idea of sending something extra, and because people tend to get a kick out of it. There's no meaning or message behind it.

You said to a fan on your facebook page that the newest book, *Commonwealth*, took, "so long and was so much work that it made me start to hate writing," can you go into more detail for us? What do you mean by that?

Oh, I meant exactly what I said. That book exhausted me. I know that it is a privilege to be a published author, but one big hardship of being an author rather than having a regular, nine-to-five job is that the work never really ends. You might be away from your computer, but you can't get your brain to stop tinkering with a certain plot point. So with Commonwealth, I'd go to bed, but after I turned out the lights, I would think, "Well, I'm lying here doing nothing. The lights are out and it's quiet so I have no distractions. This would be an ideal time to have my brain work out some details on the book—just until I fall asleep. And then, of course, the sleep wouldn't come. So, yes, writing is an art form, or a craft, but I also think of it as work, and just like with anything, if you work on the same thing so hard for so long, it will leave you soured on that particular type of work. But I took some time off from writing novels. I worked on screenplays and the freelance articles. And now I'm deep into my fourth novel, but I'm sleeping well and trying not to completely give myself over to the book.

In November, you had a short story come out that you described as, "Mad Libs meets Choose Your Own Adventure meets 21st century marketing," what can you tell us about it?

Strange career development: Mercedes needed an author to write a story, one which requires the person at the computer to enter information, so that the story becomes interactive. Because of my following in Germany, I was offered the gig. It's surprisingly dark and surreal for a story on a Mercedes site.

If you had to give one piece of advice to aspiring writers about life, not writing, what would it be?

I think the single best piece of advice I could give them would be for them to protect their health. This is something I've only recently learned myself. For instance, I've learned that exercising thirty minutes a day can help me sleep better at night. The older I get, the more I realize how if you don't have good health, you don't have much of anything. Since I've started taking better care of myself in way of diet and exercise, I've noticed that writing isn't as exruciating.

You were working on a new book this year, what can you tell us about it? Do you have a title yet?

It's set in high school and it's in first person point of view. This one has some really nice words! Nouns, verbs, a couple of prepositions—the whole deal, y'all. It's funny and sad and might be described as a geek fantasy. No title yet. I have two of the three words of the title selected. The third one keeps eluding me. Maybe "goat" will do.

How do you know when a book is "finished?"

It finally gets to the point where it becomes unhealthy to work on it anymore. I revise and revise until I just plain don't know what else to do with it.

What are three mistakes you made as a beginning writer?

One would be that I didn't always emphasize revising so much. I've learned that revising should probably take at least twice as long as drafting. Two would be that sometimes my dialogue was too "clever." I didn't notice it at the time, but re-reading some older stuff, the dialogue feels a little forced, almost cute. Thirdly, I probably wrote the word "testicles" more than was necessary.

Do you have a favorite part about being a published writer?
It has made my mother proud.

Thank you,

Goat

Bio

Joey Goebel's three novels The Anomalies, Torture the Artist, and Commonwealth, have a cult following in his own country, but it isEurope that has embraced Goebel and his "literary comedies" the most. His work is especially successful in the German domain, where he has gone on book tours and seen his novels on the best-seller list. Altogether, Goebel's novels have been published in thirteen languages.

S. G. Browne

What comes to mind when you hear, "Mourning Goats?"

Two of the three Billy Goats Gruff standing around looking at the troll as he picks pieces of the third Billy Goat from his teeth. I know, that's not how the story ends, but you asked.

Are you still "working for the man" or are you a full-time writer? What's that like?

I've managed to be a full-time writer for the past two-and a-half years, quitting my day job when my debut novel, Breathers, hit the shelves. It's good to be my own boss, but sometimes I'm kind of a slacker so my performance reports aren't always great. Still, I'm thinking about asking for a raise.

You were just at Comic-Con, what was that like?

Fun. Overwhelming. Stimulating. Lots of Hollywood celebrities and Klingon warriors and slave Princess Leias. To be honest, Comic-Con is hard to describe. It's kind of like the Matrix. No one can tell you about it. You have to see it for yourself.

I feel like you're a perfect mix of Stephen King and Chuck Palahniuk's earlier work, do you hear this reference often?

While I've had people mention Palahniuk before, I haven't had anyone bring up King. Sometimes writers cringe at comparisons, but considering that Palahniuk's Lullaby is the novel that inspired me to write Breathers and that King is the reason I wanted to become a writer, I consider it a compliment.

What was it like working in Hollywood, at Disney?

I worked post-production on the television spots and theatrical trailers for all of Disney's movies. First as a driver, then as an assistant producer – which is really just a glorified title for a project manager. The pay was good and the hours were long and you didn't get two fifteen minute breaks and you often had to work through your lunches. But when there are a thousand people who want your job, you can't really complain when you get called in at 5pm on a Sunday and have to work until 1am Monday morning without getting paid overtime. Still, I worked with a great crew and ate for free at a lot of expensive restaurants.

How excited are you about Breathers being turned into a movie?

The excitement has worn off a bit, since the project has been on a two-year spin cycle in development. When they actually green light the film, I'll get excited again.

UndeadAnonymous.com is fantastic, do you think having so much interaction with your fans is helping push the books?

I think my interactions on Facebook and Twitter have more of an impact, though I don't have any definitive data to back that up. For the most part I try to stay connected to readers while trying to maintain a balance with my writing. Which isn't always easy. The Internet has a way of sucking you in and not letting go. As for UndeadAnonymous.com, which is the official website forBreathers, I've moved most of my weekly web site interactions and updates to my website at SGBrowne.com to accommodate my other novels and work. But you can still Ask Andy a question on UndeadAnonymous.com about what it's like to be a zombie and he usually responds within a week.

What is your writing group like? Is it a bunch of published authors, friends? How often do you meet? How does it work?

It's a group of writers that have become friends over the past five years. It started out with just two of us, expanded to four, contracted, moved to San Francisco, increased to eight, and now is back down to five. Usually we meet every two weeks and workshop a book over a period of three meetings, doing 100 pages or so each meeting. The group dynamic is great at helping to work out the kinks in the books. My group has been instrumental in helping me to get my first three novels cleaned up and polished.

Have you had any interesting things happen at signings?

I had this one woman who sat with me at a signing and told me about how this guy has been stalking her for years and masturbating outside her bedroom window while barking like a dog. Apparently he showed up at the bookstore and she caught him reading a book on serial killers, which he put down as he beat a hasty retreat. She asked me if I thought she should buy the book he was reading and give it to the police to dust for fingerprints. I told her it probably wouldn't make a difference.

You give voices to things that we normally wouldn't expect, how did this come about?

I like looking at things from different angles and perspectives. I think it makes life more interesting. Even when I was writing straight supernatural horror from 1990-2002, my stories would generally evolve from the thought that whatever seemed like the truth had another reality going on. With Breathers, I liked the idea of writing from the POV of the zombie because I wondered what that would be like. Of course, I took some liberties with your standard zombie mythology, but it was fun to make the zombies the good guys and the humans the monsters.

You majored in business organization and management, how did you ever get in to writing?

This is a two-part answer. First, I was reading The Talisman by Stephen King and Peter Straub during my sophomore year in college (1985) and I got so caught up in the adventure unfolding within the pages that the world outside of the book ceased to exist. That's the first time I thought: I want to make people feel this way. Second, during that same year, I got involved in an annual event called Band Frolic, which pitted all of the living groups at my college against one another (fraternities, sororities, dorms, etc). The competition involved putting together 15-minute stage productions complete with music, dancing, and acting. I helped produce my fraternity's entry in 1986, then I was put in charge of it and for the next three years I wrote, directed, staged, and choreographed the entry for my fraternity. After two years, I knew I wanted to write. Breathers is dedicated to the fraternity brother who passed the mantle of Band Frolic director down to me. Had he not done so, I don't know if I would be answering this question right now.

Were you serious about making a reality show based on Fated?

That was actually just an idea for a short story, as I'm putting together a collection of stories to be released as an eBook and I wanted to write something based on some of the characters in Fated. The idea I came up with was to have the Seven Deadly Sins living together in a house and have it be like a reality show. But since I don't watch a lot of reality television I needed to do some research, so I watched half a dozen episodes of Jersey Shore to get some ideas. Afterwards I had my brain scrubbed.

It feels like you do a lot of research for your books, do you research before you write or in the edits?

Some writers are plotters and some are pantsers – in other words, writing by the seat of their pants. That's me. I write the same way Indiana Jones deals with Nazis and stolen artifacts – I make it up as I go. So consequently, most of my research happens as I'm writing the book when something presents itself and I realize I need more information to make the scene work. My character lives in his parents' wine cellar and drinks his way through their wine collection? I do some research on different types of expensive wine. My character has been around since the dawn of man because he's the immortal personification of Fate? I need to find out what kind of clothes he might have worn during the reign of Henry VIII. If I see something that can be improved by adding a little factual information to make it seem more realistic and potentially more humorous, then I'll add it. I enjoy doing the research. You never know what you might learn. Like how to apply make-up with either a brush or a sponge. Or that in the state of Minnesota it's illegal to have sex with a bird.

Why did you go with S. G. Browne, instead of Scott G.

Browne?

When I wrote my first story to send off for possible publication in 1990, I wrote down every permutation of my name, using full names and initials, and decided I liked the way S.G. Browne looked the best. Eighteen years later when I sold Breathers I decided to keep it that way. Hey, it worked for J.K. Rowling, right?

I read Breathers on my kindle, do you see e-books taking over anytime soon?

First of all, I want to say I appreciate it when someone reads one of my books in any format, be it electronic or trade paperback. But personally, I like books. Hard cover. Trade paperbacks. Mass-market paperbacks. I like the feel of a book in my hands. I like seeing them on my shelf. I like going into bookstores and roaming the aisles, running my fingers along spines, talking to the booksellers, getting recommendations as to what to read. It's the closest thing I get to a church. I can't get that experience searching on Amazon. It's cold and soulless out there. Unfortunately, it seems like the brick-and-mortar bookstores are in danger of disappearing from the book publishing landscape. If that happens, then I believe we will have lost an irreplaceable part of our culture.

What's the best advice you've received about writing? And, having this knowledge now, would you change anything about how you've written in the past?

The best advice I received wasn't so much about the writing process as it was about the business of writing. Specifically, Christopher Moore told me that when it comes to book signings and events: "Expect nothing and enjoy everything." I suppose that could be applied to life in general, which makes the advice that much more poignant. As to if I would change anything about how I've approached writing in the past? I don't think so. Not that I did everything right, but you don't learn from your successes as much as you learn from your mistakes. I wouldn't be who I am today without them.

I absolutely love in Breathers how on one side, the reader is disgusted by what's happening, and on the other, they're sorry for the zombie, did you plan from the beginning to write character driven novels?

One of the challenges of writing Breathers, and one of the things that drove me to write it, was to tell a story from the POV of a zombie and see if I could make the reader empathize with his condition and plight and stick by him even if he gave into his Hollywood urges. And when you're writing in first person, it's sort of natural for the novels to be more character driven. My plots definitely evolve from my characters, rather than the other way around.

Have you read anything this year that you have to tell our readers about?

The Book Thief by Markus Zusak. Not only is it the best novel I've read this year but it's one of the best novels I've ever read. Beautiful and lyrical, with a great message about the power of words.

What can you tell us about, Lucky Bastard?

Like Breathers and Fated it's a dark comedy and social satire with a supernatural or a fantastic element. In this case, the fantastic element is the fact that my main character, a private detective by the name of Nick Monday, was born with the ability to steal luck. It's set in San Francisco, takes place all in one day, and starts out on the roof of the Sir Francis Drake Hotel with a naked woman holding a butcher knife. It's got some mystery/noir elements, which is something new, and it isn't quite as overt on the social commentary as my first two novels, but I still make fun of human beings when I get the chance.

What's next for S. G. Browne? Is there any news on your short story collection?

I'm finishing up some edits on several of the short stories for the collection, which I plan to release as an eBook sometime later this year. And yes, I appreciate the irony in that considering my earlier comment about my love for books, but I also realize I can't be a complete Luddite. I'll update any news on my web site, but the collection will consist of around ten short stories that are darkly amusing, twisted tales with a dash of social satire. I'm looking forward to it. Otherwise, I'm working on my next book. All I can tell you about that right now is that it's about ego and identity and takes place in Los Angeles. Where else would a book about ego and identity take place?

How important is your education in regards to your writing?

I went to school to be a Computer Engineer, then switched to Business when I got a C- in Physics and kept falling asleep in my Thermodynamics class. I discovered my passion and desire for writing while reading Stephen King and being involved in an annual stage competition at my school in which I was in charge of writing and directing the entry for my living group. After doing that for three years, I realized I didn't want to do anything else but write. So even though I took a couple of writing classes, my classroom education played no real role in my writing. But my college experience outside of the classroom had a significant impact. Had I not been involved in that stage competition, I don't know if I'd be writing today.

How do you know when a book is "finished?"

I don't know if my books are ever finished. I could keep tinkering with them until I need dentures and Depends. But at some point you have to tell your manuscript: "Look, I know we've been spending a lot of time together lately, and I really like you, but I think we should see other people." And then you introduce your manuscript to your agent and start working on another book.

Do you have a favorite part about being a published writer?

During my sophomore year in college I was reading The Talisman by Stephen King and Peter Straub. I got so caught up in the story unfolding within the pages that the world outside of the book ceased to exist, and I thought: "I want to make someone feel this way." Years later, after publishing my first novel Breathers, I received an e-mail from someone who told me that while reading my novel, they forgot about their problems and the world outside. How can you top that? When I can connect with someone like that or make someone feel the way I set out to make myself feel, that's probably my favorite part about being a published writer.

Thank you,

Goat

Bio

S.G. Browne's debut novel, Breathers, was optioned for film by Fox Searchlight Pictures, while The Washington Post called his second book, Fated, "A terrific comic novel." His writing is inspired by his love of dark comedy, social satire, and the supernatural. His third novel, Lucky Bastard, came out in April 2012. You can visit him at www.sgbrowne.com.

Christopher Moore

What comes to mind when you hear, "Mourning Goats?"

Billy Goats Gruff.

It looks like you're doing a huge tour in 2012, what are you most excited about? Do you enjoy touring?

I do like touring. The travel is hard, but I like meeting and talking to readers. I'm not excited about any particular thing. I do have an event at the Dallas Museum of Fine Art, which will be a first for me, so that will be cool.

What do you owe your success to?

Owning what I do and continuing to do it. That is, I commit to an idea for a book and then see it through, regardless of how "unsafe" in might seem, or how unlikely it might seem as a subject for comedy.

Research seems to be very important in your novels, where do you go for most of your research?

It depends on what I'm writing about. If I'm writing about Paris, Paris. Medieval England, England. Israel, Israel. It always adds dimension to a book to go to the place where it takes place, if the events were hundreds or even thousands of years ago.

You split your time between two of the most beautiful places in the country, Hawaii and California. How do you get the motivation to lock yourself in a room and write?

Well, I'm in San Francisco almost full-time now. It's tough, to be honest. But it's what I do. It's no easier for people to go to their jobs, I don't think.

Has writing become easier for you over the years or harder, why?

The discipline of it has become harder because there are more demands on my time. That said, I have a lot more experience, so I don't have to agonize on how to resolve a scene or write a transition because I've handled so many story elements before.

Overall, I think it balances out.

Have you ever considered returning to Melancholy Cove?

I don't have a plan to do that, but I didn't have a plan to do that when I wrote the second and third book that were set there. It could happen.

How do you feel about the place of satirical and humorous fiction? Do you think they're overlooked by the literary establishment?

I do. I'm not militant about it, but it pisses me off that largely un-funny literary fiction will get much more attention than funny fiction, but, that said, there's not a lot of funny fiction.

Most if not all of your books have been optioned for films. Have you heard anything about any of them going into production?

The Stupidest Angel is supposed to start filming in April of this year. I'm not going to say for sure. We've been this close before with that one. There's a good script for A Dirty Job, but no production schedule that I know of. The other ones are still in the script development stage as far as I know.

What's it like being compared to such heavy hitters as Kurt Vonnegut and Douglas Adams?

It's flattering. I loved those guys' work. I was inspired by it.

In most interviews you bring up Cannery Row, what about it has made you return to it any time you're lost on a project?

The narrative voice. It's a very sweet voice that is forgiving toward the characters. When you write satire, it's pretty easy to start sounding bitter, so going to that gentler tone can bring the characters out and bring the reader in.

You used to live in a pretty remote area of California, with the closest bookstore being 40 miles out, have you jumped on the e-reader bandwagon as a way to easily get books to read?

I live in San Francisco. Have for almost six years. But yes, I have an e-reader, but I prefer real books. The reader is mostly for travel.

What are your thoughts on going to school for writing, at both the undergrad and graduate level? Can being a storyteller be taught?

I think it can. There are some successful writers who really swear by getting an MFA in creative writing. Others, like myself, are mostly self-taught. I think much of how much you learn is going to be how good your teachers are and what your goals are.

With tax season right around the corner, how awesome is it putting your travel, research, etc. as deductibles? Has this ever made you want to write a book about a specific area/time?

No, I've never written a book for tax reasons. I have written books because I wanted to go certain places and do certain things. Island of the Sequined Love Nun, Fluke, and my new one, Sacre Bleu, were based around subjects and locations that I wanted to learn about and travel to. Others, like Fool and Lamb, were more about the source material and subject matter, even though there was some travel involved in the research.

What do you think about writing groups? Have you ever been a part of one?

I have. They can be extraordinarily helpful and can actually help your writing get better. I have belonged to writing groups and gone to conferences and workshops and over all, they were helpful experiences.

You have over 93,000 "likes" on facebook, are you excited about breaking 100,000? What do you think facebook has done for publishing?

I'm not quite sure yet. It's moving so fast. I had about 30,000 when I tour last time, yet all of my events were huge compared to a couple of years ago. So, as far as people who are interested in my books being aware of my tour, Facebook has been huge. As far as books sales, I'm just not sure yet. We'll see, I guess. I do look forward to hitting 100,000, but I'm not sure it's a magical number or anything.

Writing satire seems to have been an accident, can you tell

us how you started in this field?

I took my horror stories to a writers' conference and read them in workshops and people laughed at them, so I thought, "Oh, this is what I do." It just turned out I had a talent for writing funny stuff, yet I really wanted to write horror, so I sort of did both. Since the first book, though, I've gone pretty far afield from horror, but there's always something supernatural in my books. I'm not sure that what I do is satire. I think satire pokes fun at a convention of the genre or at some societal element, and often my stuff is just straight comedy, without a subtext of message.

How did you get a blurb from Nicholas Sparks?

I met Nick at a bookseller's convention in Oakland when his first book was about to come out. I think it was one of his first signings and he was a little nervous. I was an old hand but that time, with my third book coming out, so as we were getting ready to sign, we started talking and I tried to be encouraging. Our agents worked in the same building, so at a later date, after Nicholas Sparks had become a household name, my agent asked him to blurb one of my books and he remembered our conversation and complied. He also chose me to go to the Today Show Book Club, as his choice, which was extraordinarily generous of him. I haven't kept in contact with him, but he's always been a very nice guy and very generous toward me.

Is it true that whales have prehensile penises?

Some of them do, yes.

What's next for Christopher Moore?

I'll tour in April 2012 for Sacre Bleu, and I'm working on a new book based on Shakespeare's work, like my book Fool.

How important is your education in regards to your writing?

My education isn't formal, but it is, of course, fundamental to the whole writing process. I'm mostly self-taught, as far as writing, and I haven't had a literature course since high-school, yet through my own efforts and some strategic extension courses and workshops I was able to develop a fairly useful set of skills.

How do you know when a book is "finished?"

I don't do a lot of rewriting, so for me, I usually know it's done when it's about a month past the time I tell my editor I'll send it in. If you're not working on deadline, then a good rule of thumb is a book is finished when you start changing stuff back to the way it was before you started to rewrite. A lot of writers will rewrite forever, letting the perfect be the enemy of the good, and never move on. If it's an early book, a writer will know more by the time he or she finishes, and that will often make a writer want to completely change the project from what it was envisioned. Often, the best think to do is make that book the best it can be as it is, and write the next one, using the new skill set, rather than trying to radically rework the project.

What are your thoughts on basing your characters on real people?

I think it's very helpful and a valid practice. I tend to do composites of several people, giving them quirks and idiosyncrasies that the real person doesn't have. It's really best to build a character who can do what you need them to do in a story, so almost invariably, if you start with a real person as model, you'll be changing them before the end of the story.

What are three mistakes you made as a beginning writer?

1) Thinking there was a short-cut to discipline of writing every day.
2) Rewriting early chapters of books before getting through the entire story.
3) Allowing the angst of "being a writer" get in the way of actually doing the work. Setting expectations so high for myself that I was paralyzed to actually get any work done. There's a weird balance of humility and hubris that a writer has to maintain to get to the page and do good work, and it took me a long time to find that balance.

Do you have a favorite part about being a published writer?

I like telling people I'm a novelist. It's a job I never have to be apologetic for. I can sit in the front row of a comedy show if I want, not worried about the comedian asking me what I do for a living. (I mean, the work is pretty terrific, although hard, but my favorite thing is just owning what I've worked so hard to achieve.)

Do you see publishing changing with all of the technological advances, today? How? Are you excited about it?

I do see it changing, but I can't be sure how it's going to go. I'm more trepidatious than excited. I think the casualty of all this instant access is our attention span, and I'm not sure the novel can compete with all the toys and distractions of the high-tech world. I find myself switching from reading something on my e-reader to watching a video or checking Twitter fairly easily, and I can't imagine that's not happening to other people. Despite the appearance of convenience, I think the multifunction e-reader — tablet or laptop — is a big box of distractions, and I don't think that bodes well for the novelist. I don't think there's anything to be done about, I just think it's a consequence of change. I like writing novels, but I'm not sure how much longer I'll be able to make a living at it, because it's going to be like writing sonnets, soon - an exercise one performs for the joy of doing it, without expectations for an audience or remuneration.

Thank you,
Goat

Bio

Christopher Moore is the author of eleven novels, including the international bestsellers, Lamb, A Dirty Job, and You Suck. His latest novel is Fool, a retelling of King Lear from the perspective of Pocket, the Fool. Chris was born in Toledo, Ohio and grew up in Mansfield, Ohio. His father was a highway patrolman and his mother sold major appliances at a department store. He attended

Ohio State University and Brooks Institute of Photography in Santa Barbara. He moved to California when he was 19 years old and lived on the Central Coast until 2003, when he moved to Hawaii. When he's not writing, Chris enjoys ocean kayaking, scuba diving, photography, and sumi-e ink painting.

Nick Hornby

What comes to mind when you hear, "Mourning Goats?"

Not to my mind, but to my eyes: I squint, to see if I've misread something about the band Mountain Goats.

What was it like having such success after your first novel?

Pretty good, for about a month. But my first book, Fever Pitch wasn't a novel, it was a memoir, and after that month I realised that I hadn't done anything, really. It's hard to keep writing memoirs, and I had a lot of my career ahead of me. The success of High Fidelity was more important to me, because it was a novel, and I was pretty sure I could write another one. I just want to work, and to feed my family through my work. The way I look at it, each book that does OK buys you the chance to write another one.

How many projects do you usually work on at a time? Does it help to have multiple things bouncing around your brain?

The way it's turned out, over the last few years, anyway, is that I've had three or four things on the go at any one time. But that doesn't mean I look at three or four things in a day, or a week, or even a month. I work on each of them until they reach their next stage, whatever, that is, and then go on to another one. At the moment I have four different movie and TV projects active, but only one of them is taking up an actual writing time at the moment. The other three are all stuck in development, at various stages. And if I were writing a novel, I'd maybe take a break from it after I'd written a third, or a half, to do a draft of something else. Screenplays are useful in that you can get a draft done in six weeks or a month, especially if it's not the first draft and you have a structure to work off. But of course, when I go to bed at night, my head's pretty chaotic. It's hard to govern what you end up thinking about.

I see you have your own writing office that isn't at home, do

you think it's important to have that kind of space that you have to "go" to?

Well, it helps me. I like the separation, the ability to leave work at the office , the walk to and fro. And if I have to do interviews, I like to meet journalists in a neutral space. I don't want my home, or my kids, to form part of an interview. It started out as a purely practical arrangement when my children were young and small and not at school, but now it's just the way things are, and always will be, for as long as I can afford it. BUT, young writers, that's not the reason your book remains unwritten. Get on with it. I couldn't afford anything outside the home for a while.

In one interview you said that you always knew you wanted to be a writer, even before you wrote, can you expand on this?

I used to think about stories a lot, even if I was too idle to write them down. And then it got to a point where they were stopping me from sleeping, and I knew I had to do something about it. It took years to get to that point, though. And I was resistant to it, I think, as well. Writing has enormous power to mess your life up.

You've written lyrics for a bunch of Ben Folds songs, what was it like working with someone across the internet? Do you think the ability to connect like this is going to bring a lot of conglomerations?

Yes, it's much easier now. I get emails out of the blue, from interesting people, and there's no way they would have sat down and written a letter to me. There's no way, either, that I would have written a letter back. So I think there's the potential for endless collaboration, or endless talk about collaboration, anyway. A lot of it comes to nothing, but so what? I loved working with Ben. It had every possibility of coming to nothing, but we were both stimulated by the challenge, and stuck at it.

What was it like selling the movie rights to Fever Pitch, twice?

It was never really exciting! The guy who directed the British movie was always convinced of its cinematic potential, even before the book was published. I thought he was nuts, and was more concerned about publication than movie rights. And we dragged on for a few years, with me writing drafts that got a little better, until Film 4 bought the rights, for a small amount of money. And actually the rights were then theirs to sell on, so there wasn't really any more. About A Boy was much more fun. I hadn't submitted it to the movie people, and I still don't know how they get hold of it, and then there was an auction. It was cool. Not real life, but fun anyway. I'm not sure if people realise this, but an enormous number of novels get optioned for the movies. If you have an idea that involves authentic-seeming people and an original narrative, then someone on the movie food chain will say they want to buy it. But that someone could be a young indie producer who doesn't have a penny to give you for it.

Do you enjoy giving readings? What should someone expect when seeing you read?

I really do, actually. I think I'm OK at it. I tend to read three or four self-contained passages from the first half of a new book, and then do a Q and A. That's the fun part, I think. That's where you can get an atmosphere going in a room.

I saw that, like a lot of authors, you don't read your reviews. With the amount of good reviews that you get, why not?

Of course, they're not all good, and even the good ones contain something that's likely to annoy me, or damage confidence in some way. Half the job is about maintaining confidence – writer's block is a crisis of confidence. So why do anything to jeopardize the little bit one has? And I don't think you can learn much from the average one thousand word review. The reviewer has spent a lot less time thinking about the book than you have, understandably, and most reviews are a couple of paragraphs of plot and a couple of paragraphs of adjectives.

In one interview you said that you're too social to want to sit

on your own for two years writing a book, is that how long it usually takes you to write a book?

Yeah, pretty much. I don't know where the time goes. The sums don't add up. I aim to do 500 to a thousand words a day when I'm up and running, which should mean I'm done in 180-odd working days. But I'm not.

Do you have someone that is your first reader for everything, or does it all depend on the material?

My wife is my first and best reader.

You were a full-time teacher and regular contributor to Esquire, the London Sunday Times, and The Independent, before becoming a novelist, what brought you to fiction?

It wasn't that way round. I was writing (unpublished and unmade) screenplays and fiction before I started doing journalism. I kind of fell into book reviewing, and then other bits and pieces, and I ended up with a column. But it was always so that I could pay for the creative writing. It was a good thing to have done, for all sorts of reasons.

Do you have a favorite book or story that you've written? Why?

Always the next one. The next one's going to be really good.

The collection The Polysyllabic Spree is a collection of 14 columns from The Believer and the proceeds are split between the Treehouse charity and a writing centre in Brooklyn, how did you get involved in these?

There are three of those collections out in the US, with a fourth due in the autumn, and the money from those tends to get given away, because I already got paid once for writing the column. TreeHouse is a school for severely autistic kids that my son attends, and 826, the literacy project founded by Dave Eggers, is very important to me,, not least because I got involved in a similar thing here, the Ministry Of Stories. I've known Dave for ten years or more, and whenever I go and see him in San Francisco, I'm always incredibly inspired by the energy and imagination of 826 and McSweeney's.

I enjoy that you want people to read your books now, and don't worry about them reading it in the future. Do you think about the legacy that you will leave in literature?

No, never. That way looks like creative death to me. In the end, books last because people read them, and really, nobody can predict whether a book will last. It's quite clear, when you read Claire Tomalin's brilliant biography of Dickens, that he didn't think about his literary immortality for a second. He was bashing things out, usually two books at once, and sometimes it's quite clear that the books suffered as a result. But would people love them more if he'd written more slowly and more carefully? It's hard to imagine. I wrote Fever Pitch because I wanted it to be read in 1992 and 1993 and I didn't think beyond that. But it's twenty years old now, and it's still in print.

It's easier than ever to find people across the internet with social media, do you believe that it's making being a writer a little less of a lonely occupation?

It doesn't matter how many friends I have on Facebook – it's still pretty quiet here during the day.

Whenever you're asked about some of your favorite writers, you mention Anne Tyler. What makes you so passionate about her writing?

She more than anybody made me want to write – she made me think it was possible. Soul, characters, humour, sadness - that's the kind of novel I aspire to.

What would you say if one of your boys comes to you in the future and says, "Dad, I want to be a writer?"

I'd be staggered. And I'd probably end up saying what everyone used to say to me: "Fine. But what are you going to do for a job?"

I think you're one of the first writer's I've read who is honest about writing to be published, not writing for yourself. Do you believe that you can do both? Write for yourself and for

money?

It's not about writing for money. The point I've tried to make is that all writers – all novelists, anyway – write with a readership in mind, whatever they say in interviews. That's why they withhold information in the narrative, and why they make jokes, and why they strive for emotional impact, and why they produce books that are roughly book length, as opposed to a million words long. They're not doing that because they imagine amusing themselves when they've finished. So to say that you're writing for yourself is disingenuous. And I've yet to meet a novelist who wanted to remain unpublished. You may be writing the kind of book that you'd want to read – I hope you are. But that's really not the same thing as "writing for yourself".

What's next for Nick Hornby?

I want to try and get these screenplays that I'm working on made – or get them into a state where they stand a chance of being made, anyway. I've been working on a series for HBO, and there will probably be more work on that, although the odds are always against production, I think, on things like that. And I've been adapting Colm Toibin's wonderful novel 'Brooklyn', too, so there will be more work on that – again, it's going to be tough to find the money for it, but I hope we can. And I'm just beginning to think about a novel set in the 1960s.

Thank you,
Goat

Bio

Nick Hornby is the author of the bestselling novels Slam, A Long Way Down, How to Be Good, High Fidelity, and About a Boy, and the memoir Fever Pitch. He is also the author of Songbook, a finalist for a National Book Critics Circle Award, Shakespeare Wrote for Money, and The Polysyllabic Spree, and editor of the short story collection Speaking with the Angel. A recipient of the American Academy of Arts and Letters' E. M. Forster Award, and the Orange Word International Writers' London Award 2003, Hornby lives in North London.

PERFECT
EDGE
BOOKS

We live in uncertainty. New ways of committing crimes are discovered every day. Hackers and hit men are idolized. Writers have responded to this either by ignoring the harsher realities or by glorifying mindless violence for the sake of it. Atrocities (from the Holocaust to 9/11) are exploited in cheaply sentimental films and novels.

Perfect Edge Books proposes to find a balanced position. We publish fiction that doesn't revel in nihilism, doesn't go for gore at the cost of substance — yet we want to confront the world with its beauty as well as its ugliness. That means we want books about difficult topics, books with something to say.

We're open to dark comedies, "transgressive" novels, potboilers and tales of revenge. All we ask is that you don't try to shock for the sake of shocking — there is too much of that around. We are looking for intelligent young authors able to use the written word for changing how we read and write in dark times.